DIARY
OF A JOB
SEARCH

DIARY
OF A JOB
SEARCH

ONE MAN'S JOURNEY FROM
UNEMPLOYMENT TO A NEW CAREER

TIM JOHNSTON WITH LAURA LORBER AND PERRI CAPELL

TEN SPEED PRESS

BERKELEY / TORONTO

Ten Speed Press
Box 7123
Berkeley, California 94707
www.tenspeed.com

Distributed in Australia by Simon & Schuster Australia, in Canada by Ten Speed Press Canada, in New Zealand by Southern Publishers Group, in South Africa by Real Books, and in the United Kingdom and Europe by Airlift Book Company.

Cover and text design by Ed Anderson
Cover photograph by Rick Luettke

Portions of this material originally appeared in electronic form on the website of CareerJournal.com, property of The Wall Street Journal Online Network, Princeton, New Jersey.

Library of Congress Cataloging-in-Publication Data

Johnston, Tim.
    Diary of a job search : one man's journey from unemployment to a new career / Tim Johnston with Laura Lorber and Perri Capell.
        p. cm.
Includes index.
    ISBN 1-58008-545-8
    1. Job hunting—United States. I. Lorber, Laura. II. Capell, Perri.
III. Title.
    HF5382.75.U6 J64 2003
    650.14—dc22

Printed in the United States
First printing, 2003

1 2 3 4 5 6 7 8 9 10—07 06 05 04 03

DEDICATION

Writing about losing my job started as a catharsis: it was just a chance for me to vent. By the time the first article was published online, I had already written five or so pieces and had fallen into a groove. Once the accompanying online discussion started rolling, I was surprised by how gratified I was to learn that many other job seekers shared my fears, frustrations, and silly thoughts. I felt their support so much that at times it didn't matter to me if I ever did find a job. To those who took the time to write and share, thank you. And thank you for helping me to always remember that I was not alone.

—Tim Johnston

CONTENTS

ACKNOWLEDGMENTS

It seems somehow odd to acknowledge others for help with a "diary," yet this diary truly would not have happened without quite a bit of help. To Tony Lee, Laura Lorber, Perri Capell, and the other great folks at CareerJournal.com, thanks for your support and your excellent writing, and for making this book happen. (Anthony Catalano, thanks for manning the discussion board!) Niels Nielsen, thank you for making the articles possible by suggesting to Laura Lorber that I might be the right jobless soul for the gig. Mom, Dad, and sister Sarah, thank you for providing me with a deep well to draw upon. To my in-laws, Sue Levin and Lee Rosenson, thanks for the love, food, and housing while we were off our feet. To my daughter, Hannah, thank you for your joyful presence. And to my wife, Claire Rosenson, thanks for your professional editing skills and your support for this project, and especially for seeing the loss of my job as an exciting opportunity from the moment I called you and told you I'd been laid off. I love you.

—Tim Johnston

FOREWORD

Tim Johnston's story contains all of the elements of the classic American novel: an empathetic hero who faces adversity, rises to meet his challenges, suffers numerous setbacks, then finally achieves his goal and rides off into the sunset. Tim's tale is both heartwarming and instructive. But unlike Tim, many unemployed executives these days aren't sharing such a happy ending.

When we launched Tim's "Diary of a Job Search" on CareerJournal.com, we were astounded by the response from readers. While hundreds sent us emails and discussion board postings with suggestions for Tim and synopses of their own successful strategies, the most common response was, "Me too." Tim's column had struck a chord, and unemployed executives, managers, and professionals around the world wrote to tell us about their unwanted, extended job searches.

"I thought I was all alone until I read Tim's story" was the most common posting. "Just knowing that I'm not unique in my suffering is a great help." Tim's fluid writing style and great sense of humor captured the hearts of his readers. They saw him as an embodiment of the recession's impact on managerial careers. It soon became clear that for every job seeker like Tim, there were hundreds of unsung jobless and underemployed professionals who longed for the chance to contribute through challenging, meaningful jobs.

In *Diary of a Job Search*, Tim offers helpful suggestions in every chapter; these are bolstered with additional insights from editors Laura Lorber and Perri Capell. But perhaps the most critical lesson that resonates throughout the book is the power of networking. The act of telling everyone you know about your job search, then telling everyone they know until you uncover a relevant job opportunity, remains the single most effective method of identifying a new job. This makes sense, especially when you consider that employee referrals—candidates who are hired because they were recommended by a current employee—are the number-one source of new hires at most companies.

In fact, it was through networking that we came to know Tim. Once we developed the idea of chronicling one executive's job search during these turbulent times, we set about trying to find just the right author, and it was a recommendation from the leader of a local job club that helped us identify Tim as the perfect candidate.

With help like this from our many friends, we've been very fortunate at CareerJournal.com. The site launched in 1997 as the logical evolution of another job-search guide: the *National Business Employment Weekly,* a tabloid newspaper I oversaw for eight years. During that time, the *NBEW* served as the only timely source of career-guidance information in the country. While local newspapers and business magazines occasionally published an article about the status of the job market, the *NBEW* chronicled a sea change in how people manage their careers, led by the baby-boom generation of young managers and salaried employees.

Now that those boomers have reached the executive suite in greater numbers, a fair share have struggled with dilemmas their parents typically never had to consider: balancing two incomes with child-rearing, overcoming the stereotypes and glass ceilings of corporate America, and learning to develop younger colleagues to whom the boomers had never given a second thought. CareerJournal.com is dedicated to helping you understand and synthesize these issues as you develop your career within a big or small company or one that you own.

Tim's story is an inspirational tale from which we can all learn. He shows that through constructive self-analysis, persistence, a sense of humor, and hard work, you can fulfill your career ambitions.

—Tony Lee, editor in chief/general manager, CareerJournal.com

PREFACE

This book is a collaboration between former job hunter Tim Johnston and us, the editors of CareerJournal.com. It grew out of Tim's column, "Diary of a Job Search," which we published in installments starting in April 2002 and continuing until November 2002.

Between the two of us, we have been writing and editing job-search and career-management advice for nearly twenty years, first, at the *National Business Employment Weekly* and then at CareerJournal.com, which is *The Wall Street Journal's* site for executives, managers, and professionals with career concerns. Although we offer more than three thousand articles on topics such as résumé preparation, interviewing, pay-negotiation strategies, and other career-related issues and trends, something was missing.

As editors, we had long wanted to run a series of articles chronicling the ups and downs of one executive's path to reemployment, but the right person who could create this "Diary of a Job Search" hadn't surfaced. We needed an executive willing to share the intimate details of what likely would be one of the most difficult and uncertain periods of his or her life—someone who was willing to honestly tackle the tough subjects. Most important, that person should be someone who could articulate these issues as they arose—in short, someone who could write well on a tight deadline while also conducting a job hunt.

When the job market went south, the idea for the series resurfaced, and we renewed our effort to pursue it. We asked career advisers nationwide if they could refer job seekers who might fit the bill. Consultant Niels Nielsen, who has run a job-seekers club in Princeton, New Jersey, for the past thirty years, gave us seven names. At the top of the list was Tim Johnston's, and Niels said he'd likely be our man.

We called Tim and made our pitch. After we chatted a bit, we asked him to send his résumé and a writing sample that recounted how his search got started and how he'd arrived at this current phase of his life. After reading his first attempt, we knew we'd gotten lucky and found our columnist. That writing sample became "Absorbing the Shock of Losing Your Job," the first installment of the thirteen-part series.

The column was an immediate success with readers. The first day it appeared, Tim received more than thirty emails, most of them messages of support. At this point, we created a discussion board on CareerJournal.com devoted to the column. This allowed readers to share their comments and exchange tips and words of encouragement. The discussion quickly took on a life of its own, and several participants even started recounting their own job-search struggles. Most who wrote thanked Tim for helping them understand they weren't alone. The following is a typical post:

I found Tim's article and the subsequent discussion on the board informative and strangely comforting. It's less isolating to realize that others share the experience of these difficult times. —Kofi D.

The discussion-board community continued and grew throughout Tim's search. In fact, his Diary continues to be an inspiration to readers, which is our motivation for wanting to reach an even wider audience through the publication of this book.

Diary of a Job Search is more than Tim's story: it also includes job-search guidance that we've gleaned over the years as editors of CareerJournal.com. Each chapter of the book recounts Tim's search as it unfolds, followed by a job-hunter's primer of sorts. On the premise that those experiencing an ordeal—or who have successfully survived one—are often the best teachers, we've also included some of the tips and suggestions that readers posted to the discussion board about their searches. (Discussion-board participants are identified by their screen name; if they listed their full name, we've used only their first name and last initial here to protect their privacy.) In a sense, the book is a collaboration between Tim, the editors of CareerJournal.com, and America's unemployed.

We believe that Tim's job-hunt story resonates with readers because, in a sense, he's a white-collar Everyman. As you read this book, we hope you gain from his experience and the guidance offered herein, and that they help ease the travails of your own job search.

—Laura Lorber and Perri Capell

CHAPTER 1

ABSORBING THE SHOCK OF
LOSING YOUR JOB

- Throwing out the Old Rules
- Emotional Recovery
- Warning Signs
- Your Layoff Plan
- Updating Your Résumé
- Negotiating Severance Pay
- Applying for Unemployment
- Evaluating Your Finances
- A Sensible Search Strategy
- How to Start Networking

February 16

On January 8, at 3:35 p.m., I lost my job with a Boston nonprofit. I expected the layoff, but not the subtle shock that set in over subsequent weeks as I realized how much the world had changed since my last job search.

I'd spent fifteen years in a variety of disparate and often concurrent occupations—consultant/programmer, theater director, university administrator, voice-over artist, and others—choosing jobs and projects that offered new areas for learning and a chance to create something from the ground up. Then I had an epiphany. A master's degree in business administration would help me connect all of these experiences and fill in gaps in my knowledge. In 1998, my wife, Claire, and I moved from North Carolina to Boston, where I earned my M.B.A. at Boston University. I collected a second master's degree in management information systems simultaneously, since it was only a few bucks more.

When I graduated in May 2000, anyone who could breathe could get a job. I accepted a position as marketing director for a nonprofit that created web-based courses for physicians. Then dot-coms started collapsing and the recession began. Scores of my classmates found themselves unemployed. The nonprofit world, by contrast, seemed stable. But when future funding suddenly became uncertain, my position was eliminated.

At first, Claire and I were relieved. We'd grown weary of Boston for several reasons. It was too expensive. We had few close friends and little time to make new ones. And we now had a child. Our daughter, Hannah, was almost a year old. Suddenly free, we could relocate to New Jersey (Exit 8, if you're asking), where we both have family.

A FRESH START

Just a few years ago, returning to New Jersey would have felt like a form of failure to me. Having a child changed that. Being physically close to family again seemed like a wonderful completion, a return to wholeness.
I grew up in Princeton, where my father and sister still live. Claire's father and stepmother live close by, and assorted other sisters, stepbrothers, aunts, uncles, cousins, and so on, live within a fifty-mile radius. Hannah would have playmates; we'd have support, comfort, and (we hoped) occasional free childcare.

By moving day, we were so anxious to leave for the Promised Land that I didn't even argue with the movers when they told me I had to saw the legs off our sofa to get it out of our house. Apparently, furniture's physical properties can change over time. Though the sofa went in with legs, they had to come off to remove it. I bought a saw around the corner and cut off the legs.

So, within four weeks of losing my job, we'd jammed our stuff into storage in New Jersey and taken up residence in my in-laws' house, bringing only a small quantity of clothes, job-search materials, and Hannah's toys for "the occupation." Having fled Boston successfully, I was ready to begin my job search in earnest.

But now I'm beginning to realize that the world is very different from when I last sought work eighteen months ago. It's different because of fatherhood, technology, the recession, and September 11. As I crank up my search to a furious pitch from my in-laws' dining room, I start to recognize these factors and their impact.

Now that I'm a father, I see every consequence of unemployment—real and imagined—in terms of how it affects my daughter. For example, Claire and I cried when we took Hannah out of her beloved day-care center in Boston.

IS ANYBODY OUT THERE?

The evolution of the Internet as a recruiting and hiring channel (by one estimate, there are forty thousand job sites) has made establishing human contact with potential employers far more difficult. Charm and presence, which I've always perceived to be among my strong assets, are suddenly difficult to apply. Now when I make a cold call to an employer, I hit a more solid wall. The larger the company, the harder it is to get even a name of a contact.

"Can you tell me the name of the person responsible for hiring?" is met with "Why do you want to know?" Up to this point, I'm fine. A small joke or a little warmth and I should be set.

"Well, I'm very interested in learning more about how your company does [fill in the blank]," I say with a smile.

"Just send your résumé to recruiting@company.com."

"Well, I'd like to make it more personal. Can you help me with a name?"

"No." End of conversation. I'm still trying to follow up with several Sirs or Madams.

The recession and the general numbing effect of the events of September 11 have created a buyer's market in which I'm one of eight thousand candidates for almost any job. Everyone also seems a little depressed, unsure, and suspicious because of the new circumstances. As I soak up these emotions through my cold calls, I'm not feeling too well myself. I hang on Alan Greenspan's every word.

After three weeks of sending hastily updated résumés into the electronic void and trying to follow up with the nameless people who received them, I realize no movement will happen without serious networking, because networking has become exponentially more important. While family surrounds me, it dawns on me that, after an eighteen-year absence, I may not know anyone else in New Jersey. I'm home and yet I'm not. I don't know who's hiring or even which companies are in the area.

RECONNECTING

I've been trying to make a list of people I know, but it isn't easy, especially when I'm down. (David Rockefeller has an index card for everyone he's ever met; I wish I'd started doing this years ago.) The more contacts the better, so I try to identify people with whom I have the smallest connection. In this respect, the Internet is a big help. You can learn almost everything about someone, as long as you're not choosy about who that someone is. So I'm hoping to get lucky by contacting people I'm connected with in some small way; for example, "I see from your online profile that we both like cats . . . So, what do you do for a living?"

Trying to build my network, I hit up my dad for contacts. He's had a long and successful consulting career. We quickly realize, however, that he has scant experience with networking circa 2002. He thinks I want to talk with people who can directly hire me. He used to just "go and see some people" to find work. After dinner out one night, we go to his house. Sitting around the dining-room table, I wonder if his Christmas-card list might yield gold. He's pretty sure that he doesn't know anyone who can help, insisting that, since he's 73, most everyone he ever knew is dead. I start going through the list.

"What about this one?" I ask. "Oh, he's a good connection . . . but he's half-dead." "Is he half-dead or all dead?" I probe. Once I stress that I simply need names of people who will take my call because I mention his name, things proceed more smoothly. Turns out there are some people who can help me who also happen to be living.

Now I just have to rework my résumé so that recipients will understand how I can create value for them. Gotta get busy . . .

THROWING OUT THE OLD RULES

Welcome to the world of Tim, the job hunter. After he loses his position at a nonprofit in Boston and relocates his family to New Jersey, almost everything is new to him. Coupled with the shock of losing his job, this is a major upheaval that ranks high on the list of life's major stressors. Since you're reading this book, you know what we're talking about.

When Tim wrote his series for CareerJournal.com, the U.S. job market had just done a radical about-face. Just about anyone who wanted to could find a job during the go-go years lasting from the mid-1990s to 2000. Then the bottom dropped out. The Internet bubble burst, terrorists attacked the United States, financial scandals rocked Enron and other Fortune 500 companies, and consumer buying power could no longer stave off recession (recovery prospects were further dampened when the United States went to war with Iraq in March 2003).

The combined economic and geopolitical problems led to massive layoffs and business failures in the United States. Talented executives and professionals lost jobs en masse. Unemployment climbed steadily. Enter Tim with his job-search chronicles, generating an outpouring of sentiment on the Career-Journal.com website.

Clearly, it was going to be harder for Tim and other people searching for jobs during this period. But their circumstances can't be ascribed to bad luck. Rather, it's the luck of the draw. Nowadays, there's no control over when you lose a job. However, you do have control over how you find one. Surveys and anecdotal research have shown that certain techniques of job hunting work better than others. To hone their skills, many professionals have sought out the help of career counselors. There are many to choose from, as career counseling has become a sizable U.S. industry since the 1980s. Whether or not you choose to do this is a personal decision and can depend on your personal circumstances and financial resources.

The first step, however, is to process your job loss and the emotions that result. Until you are reconciled to what happened, your feelings will resemble an invisible anchor tied to your waist. They'll hold you back.

EMOTIONAL RECOVERY

Tim felt relief about his job loss, for several reasons. Others don't normally feel this way. Losing a job can make you feel shell-shocked. It isn't uncommon to become numb; some professionals feel almost paralyzed. Take time to lick your wounds, but not too long. There will be a period of grieving—just make it as short as possible.

Some job seekers wrote to the CareerJournal.com discussion board asking for advice on dealing with their feelings of anger and resentment. And readers responded. In this posting, one reader shares how she felt after her job loss and the process she used to repair her attitude:

I was laid off from a job that was just right, where I was very well-respected and where I was able to grow and learn. It was completely and utterly against my plans to leave. It was just so wrong.

I think that time is the only thing that can really make you get over it: Move on. Look at the new opportunities opening up for you. In whatever job the future holds for you, get as much out of it for yourself as the company gets out of it from you. Look at every job as a transition to something new. Everything is temporary, just like life. Make sure now is worth it. Give and give more, yet be more selfish.

I think you really have to fight the bitterness—probably every day for quite some time. Just know that you can fight it. It may have ruined your immediate past, but don't let it ruin your future. Forget about what actually happened that caused the layoff—whoever was right or wrong, whoever said this or that. There is a good chance that it matters only to you—and you can let that work to your advantage. A new employer is going to want to know what you can do for it in the future. So let the future be your focus. —Meena

WARNING SIGNS

Tim saw his job loss coming and so perhaps was a bit more prepared for the blow when it came than are those who don't anticipate it. So how do you know that a layoff or firing is imminent? An obvious sign is a bad performance review. Some signals are more subtle, such as losing your prized parking spot or other perk. Such warnings usually are sounded long before the dreaded event actually occurs. These can include the following:

- Reassignment of your primary responsibilities
- A change of attitude or demeanor in your boss or colleagues, especially those "in the know"
- Exclusion from key meetings
- A request to train new hires for your job
- A hint (or written warning) from your supervisor

I was shocked when I was laid off last year, though I knew things were really bad at the company for which I worked. Sales were down probably 50 percent from the prior year. I just never thought I would be the one who got voted off the island. In retrospect, I can see that I was just choosing not to see reality. —uptown123

In many circumstances, there's an announcement or rumor of a merger, acquisition, or other reorganization. If you've heard one, learn what you can about possible overlaps in responsibilities. Will the new entity need more or fewer people in your area? Is a new management team putting its own people into key roles, while long-time employees are losing their jobs?

Discussion-board participants compiled their own list of warning signs:

- "When the president cries in a company meeting."
- "The company keeps rearranging cubes and moving people around."
- "The company talks about new processes and procedures that we all must follow to make our jobs easier and more efficient."
- "The company keeps hiring contractors with not enough jobs for workers."
- "You are told, 'We're not cutting staff' and then your manager looks you in the eye and says 'Don't worry.'"
- "You walk into your boss's office, and he/she is looking for a job on Monster.com."

- "You have to go through mountains of paperwork just to get a new pen in the office."
- "When projects are constantly cancelled or the scopes of the projects change on a weekly basis."

Managers are often in a good position to sense early-warning signs. This job seeker gave the CareerJournal.com discussion board a recap of the red flags he saw at his company:

I was lucky in my situation. Being fairly high in the "food chain" as a director of planning with my former company, I got to see the troubles coming long before they hit my job. My former job responsibilities included providing health and status reports for my division. Those weekly and monthly reports contained a litany of lost proposals, technical problems, and cost overruns. In addition, we had a new parent company whose "hands-off" year was almost up. I knew that reorganization and job cuts were probably coming in January.

In late December, I found out the last straw when the Pentagon announced cancellation of a Navy program, for which my old company was a major participant. As expected, during the first week of January, the parent company announced that our division would be merged into another company they had just procured, eliminating entire departments and, by the end of January, my job. —John I.

YOUR LAYOFF PLAN

Perhaps because of Tim's subtle mental preparation, he was able to plan a job-search strategy with relative speed and begin to execute it within a few weeks. If you sense a job loss is near, create a plan for your layoff before the pink slip comes. By keeping a cool head and evaluating your options, you'll be better prepared than most. Your plan should include these steps:

1. Update your résumé (see chapter 3 for much more about this)
2. Reconnect with your network
3. Negotiate a severance package (if possible)
4. Apply for unemployment
5. Assess your finances
6. Launch a job search

When the layoff happens, don't argue with your boss. The decision has been made. There's no point in making an appeal unless you have real reason to believe that you're being unfairly discriminated against. In exit interviews, stay on good terms with your former employer and arrange for references. If your employer offers outplacement services or career counseling, take it. Do likewise if you're offered an office with a desk and computer to use while you're job hunting.

There's no time to waste, as one job seeker reader counseled another on the discussion board:

If you really believe job cuts are in the wings, lay the groundwork for your search now. Get your résumé in order. Begin to discreetly network and search for opportunities. You have four months that you can't afford to waste. This market is tight. Don't lose time. The longer you are out after the layoff period, the greater your momentum will suffer. Be energetic now. Start the search. —Mike

UPDATING YOUR RÉSUMÉ

Ideally, you should be updating your résumé continually regardless of whether a job loss is imminent, dutifully adding accomplishments and promotions as they occur. If, like most folks, you've let it slide, now is the time to shake off the dust. If you know where you've stored the most recent rendition, you won't have to start completely from scratch. But you're actually better off creating an entirely new document instead of adding new jobs to the old one, especially if it's been years since you last looked for a job. Rewriting your career history will give you a fresh presentation and reacquaint you with past accomplishments.

Where do you start? Realize first that a résumé isn't a job description. Listing every past employer isn't necessary or helpful. A résumé should describe the specific experience related to the role you're seeking, plus your training and education. It may be sufficient (and help to minimize age issues) to include only the roles you've held for the past decade, leaving out early career jobs.

Many job hunters are qualified for related, yet distinctly different, openings. It's to their advantage to create different versions of their résumés suited to the various jobs they may seek. Each version should highlight certain aspects of your experience.

The purpose of a résumé is to get you an interview, so consider it a marketing document. Think in terms of your features and attributes and why an employer could benefit from hiring you. As executive recruiters like to say, a candidate's past performance is the best indicator of his or her future performance, so highlight your contributions to your past employers. Explain how you helped to achieve important goals, such as boosting revenues and profits, improving product or service quality, increasing operating efficiencies, or reducing costs. Whenever possible, use numbers to measure these contributions.

To stand out in today's world of email and optical scanners, your résumé must contain the buzzwords of your industry. Be sure to pepper your document with keywords, those nouns or short phrases—such as "project management," "M.B.A.," or "UNIX"—that an employer might use to search for candidates in an electronic résumé database.

Looks count, but only to the extent that your document is neat, professional looking, and easy to read. Don't agonize over fonts and formats. You'll need both a print and an electronic version of your résumé. The paper version is your primary marketing document. Choose a good bond paper in a conservative color—such as white, ivory, or light gray—and use a sharp-looking serif typeface such as Times Roman. Your electronic version should use plenty of white space and be saved as a plain-text document.

A final but important step: Proofread your résumé. Put it aside for a day and proofread it again. Ask a friend or colleague to reread it for errors. Mistakes on a résumé can be deadly. A single error will overshadow the facts about you and leave a lasting negative impression with employers. For more on writing an effective resume, see chapter 3.

NEGOTIATING SEVERANCE PAY

If you learn that a downsizing is in the works, find out what, if anything, your employer typically offers in severance pay. Someone in your employer's human-resources or employee-benefits department should know. If you can, find out the size of the largest packages offered to employees. Learn about the standards in your industry by calling a trade group or professional association. They often conduct surveys showing the typical payments offered by companies in your field. This knowledge will help if you end up in negotiations with your employer.

If you're offered severance pay when you're laid off, ask questions and focus on understanding your options. Don't react on the basis of your emotions. Be prepared with alternatives that might help you to bargain for more. If you've lost your job in a mass layoff, you're unlikely to receive special treatment. In fact, severance isn't negotiable in most cases. An average package includes two weeks' pay for every year you've been with the company up to a ceiling. Senior managers typically receive one month's pay for each year of service.

If you feel the package you're offered is unfair, you may be able to negotiate if the circumstances of your dismissal were unusual. You don't necessarily need a lawyer to get a better deal. (If you want to maintain a good relationship with your former employer, it may be smarter to represent yourself. You can ask a lawyer for advice prior to any meetings or to review your offer.) Those dismissing you may feel a sense of guilt. You can leverage their short-term concern to gain concessions that can smooth your way through unemployment. The following are points that could be negotiated:

- If you're due an annual bonus, the company may be able to give you a prorated amount.
- If you're due stock options, request an accelerated vesting period so you can exercise them now.
- Depending on how your pension or deferred compensation plan payments are calculated, if you're close to retirement age, ask to have more years added to your length of service or age on a one-time basis so that you can meet the minimum amount required to receive full retirement payments.
- Ask to keep your office space and phone line while you job hunt.
- Find out whether you can buy your company car at a discount and keep your computer free of charge.
- Seek job-search assistance from a reputable outplacement firm.

You may have more bargaining power than you realize—employers want to avoid negative publicity and don't like disgruntled former employees contacting board members, the media, or government agencies. But to get a significantly better deal, you'll have to make a case that your layoff is a gross injustice and possibly illegal. Again, you may need to talk with a lawyer to determine whether your concerns are justified.

Negotiation is a two-way street. Focus on the needs and desires of your employer as well as your own. The following tips may help:

- Negotiate with someone with decision-making authority
- Be patient
- Don't be intimidated by a deadline
- Set a realistic goal; compromise will make a "win-win" solution possible
- Be persistent
- Stress the fairness of your proposal
- Don't be embarrassed to discuss your economic hardships, the harm done to your family, and your loss in income, benefits, and retirement savings
- Prepare a list of accomplishments and emphasize your years of service and the profits you've helped earn for the company

You may have a choice between receiving your severance pay as a lump sum or in weekly payments. Above all, don't take a lump sum and blow it on a long vacation. Most folks are better off receiving weekly payments and starting a job search immediately. After you find a new position, you can always negotiate a later start date and then unwind on an overdue vacation. Plus, if you receive weekly payments, your health-insurance benefits may be continued for the same period.

APPLYING FOR UNEMPLOYMENT

Executives are sometimes embarrassed to file for unemployment. They fear someone might see them. You'll do better to forget your ego. Your tax dollars have gone into the fund; now it's your turn to receive the benefits. You may not even have to show up in person to apply for the checks; in many states, you can apply for benefits through the mail, over the phone, by fax, or via the Internet.

Maximum benefits range from $200 to more than $400 weekly. The money won't necessarily cover the mortgage, but it can put food on the table. You can collect at least twenty-six weeks of benefits, but those weeks don't have to be consecutive. In fact, many states will reward you for working part time.

To collect, you must have worked for an employer who has contributed to the state unemployment fund, and you must have lost your job through no fault of your own; you must be able and available to work and be actively seeking work. You usually have to report your status every two weeks or so by either phoning in or filling out a form. A word to the wise: unemployment insurance is taxed as regular income. Make sure to ask Uncle Sam to withhold those taxes. Otherwise, you'll face an unexpected tax bill the following April.

Several states offer job-search-assistance programs tailored specifically for professionals. These usually are run by members of volunteer organizations and are worth investigating. You may be able to attend seminars on networking, interviewing, salary negotiations, résumés and cover letters, word processing, and using the Internet. Computers, faxes, copiers, and telephones may also be available.

EVALUATING YOUR FINANCES

Assess your financial requirements early. Start by having an honest discussion with your spouse or partner about your finances and reemployment plans. It's important that you enlist your partner's support.

List all sources of monthly income and all monthly expenses. If you're receiving severance pay, you may not have to make drastic changes to your lifestyle immediately. But plan for the time when this will run out.

John I. shared how he and his wife planned for his impending layoff:

When I received my annual bonus in December, instead of buying gifts my wife and I used it to wipe out short-term debts. Last September, my wife had retired from her job with a mortgage broker, but as the troubles at my job mounted, I encouraged her to get her old job back, which she did in January. In addition, we looked at our regular expenses carefully and cut them where possible.

To its credit, my old company and its parent offered a very generous severance package. The normal package was a week for every year of service, but in this reorganization, they doubled the severance and extended health benefits for nine months following the layoff. From the early days when our company was privately held and had no severance program, I had accumulated twelve weeks of vacation and sick time to go with the eighteen weeks of severance being offered for my nine years of service. Despite having to take the tax hit of receiving the severance and vacation pay in a lump sum, I received a comfortable amount of money to tide me over while I began my search for a new job . . . I've had a few close calls for a new job, but so far, good fortune hasn't been mine. But at least the money is holding out well.

A SENSIBLE SEARCH STRATEGY

Don't panic and send out a flurry of résumés. Likewise, don't plunge into dialing up all your networking contacts until you know what you want them to help you with. Create a job-search plan. It should include all of these elements:

- Networking
- Online job hunting
- Industry research
- Job fairs
- Information interviews
- Contacting recruiters or temporary agencies
- Additional training (if needed)

Expect your hunt to take time. According to one long-cited rule of thumb, you'll need to spend at least a month for every $10,000 in annual salary you earned at your last job.

For starters, make yourself available for interviews (another reason to forgo the vacation). Be open to taking temporary assignments.

Choose friends to confide in. Most of us develop close ties to coworkers, who can become as near and dear as actual family. Don't reinforce your sense of loss by isolating yourself from them and other professional acquaintances. Network actively and be open to making new friendships with people you meet. Set aside time to socialize and stay connected. Being alone too much can increase feelings of anxiety and depression during a job search.

HOW TO START NETWORKING

While you might prefer to hide in a closet, it's important to be visible. Networking works. Job seeker Paul V. bears witness to this statement:

After thirty years and six jobs in telecom, I've found all but one through networking. It seems that a common associate of both job candidates and hiring authorities is the most effective job-hunting tool. The common associate doesn't have anything of major significance to gain from the introduction and that's what both parties seem to trust. I would never dissuade an individual from pursuing other methods of job hunting, but give it the proper weight of your limited time.

Start by meeting with people you know on a first-name basis and are certain will respond to any requests you might make. These are the folks with whom you feel most relaxed. If you see a layoff coming, start reconnecting with your network right away. Be sure to take home your Rolodex and a copy of your email address book in case you're not allowed access to your office after the deed is done. When it comes to networking, more is always better. Contacts can include:

- Former colleagues and bosses
- Friends and neighbors
- Family members
- Fellow alumni and former professors
- Members of your church or synagogue
- Members of recreational, athletic, or other groups to which you belong
- Fellow job seekers (join a job-search support group)
- Just about anyone you encounter

When you're networking, don't come right out and ask for a job. Rather, seek information about your industry and which companies are growing and changing. Aim to come away with two names of other people you can follow up with. Request twenty minutes in the office—*not* over lunch or a drink—your contacts should meet you in a business environment, so they can see you as a professional.

Networking without a predetermined goal is ineffective; your contacts will be frustrated because they won't know how to help you. So set goals for each meeting—for instance, securing two referrals or information about a new industry development. And don't overstay your welcome at an appointment; keep that twenty-minute window in mind and discreetly check a wall clock or your watch; be aware, too, of any indicators from your contact that it's time to wrap up.

When talking with contacts, never criticize former employers. Know what you want to say so you won't be caught off guard; try to provide contacts with useful information you may have gained during your job search. Immediately after each meeting, send a handwritten thank-you note to the contact. And don't call the same person too frequently.

Don't try to do too much too quickly or overschedule yourself—if you don't get results from your exhaustive efforts, you'll get discouraged.

Aside from the isolation and financial concerns, the worst part of unemployment is often the toll it takes on one's self-esteem. No one can adequately understand the emotional roller-coaster it will take you on unless they've experienced it firsthand. If you're anticipating a layoff, you can help preserve your self-esteem and maintain a sense of control by taking action now—and by knowing that you're not alone.

●   ●   ●

You are not the only one going through this. Countless professionals with excellent credentials have been laid off and are having difficulty finding a new job. Don't doubt that you are a valuable person and that you'll find satisfying work.

CHAPTER 2

WHAT TO DO WHEN OPTIONS ABOUND

February 28

Job-search experts say that the key to success in any job search is to know exactly what kind of work you want to do. They also advise that job seekers select their positions carefully to reduce job-hopping. These are fine ideas. Last year, I'd tell out-of-work friends: "Take time to figure out who you really want to be. Choose your next job carefully. Enjoy the time off, because you won't have this flexibility again."

Now that I'm unemployed, I just want a damn job.

Figuring out exactly what kind of work you want to do is a great idea. But what if you're happy doing any number of things? At my core, I'm a generalist. I like challenges, like to solve complex problems, build something, and then move on to the next thing. Give me your nastiest challenge, the one that keeps you awake at night, and let me go—I love it. I know precisely what I want to do; I'm just not sure where and for whom.

I decided that I should follow my own advice. About a week after I was laid off back in January, I completed an online career assessment. The results showed that my strongest interests are in communications, business administration and management, entertainment, information management and analysis, and social service. Wow. This was an eye-opener that really narrowed the choices for me. I've worked in all of these fields, and I've always liked many different types of work.

Because of my diverse experience, the process of creating a fifteen-second elevator pitch is absolutely excruciating. Any particular one must omit 80 percent of my experience. A few days ago I tried a pitch on several fellow job seekers at a local job club I've joined. It was general enough to capture all my experience. "I'm an entrepreneur and intrapreneur, who likes to create or build ventures and programs using my leadership, consulting, marketing, and IT skills." Their interest was piqued. "What's an intrapreneur?" they each asked. (For the uninitiated, intrapreneurs advance independent, innovative projects as employees within a corporate environment.)

TOO MANY CHOICES

Since I don't want to limit my search to a single industry or function, I've been applying for jobs that seem to use my most saleable skills. If I were twenty-seven and single, consulting would be perfect for me, because it uses everything I've got. But now that I have a child, I can't imagine spending 50 to 90 percent of my nights away from home. Most recently, I was director of marketing and business development for a nonprofit that creates Web-based courses for physicians. So I'm sending résumés to companies that do pharmaceutical marketing, technology-based education, and consulting. So far, I'm not having much luck. The problem seems to be that employers look at what I've done in their industry and are puzzled by my other experience. I can't leave it out, or I'd have years missing from my résumé. Can I say I was traveling?

My fellow job seekers and a career counselor I've spoken with say I have to do a better job of "connecting the dots" for hiring managers. I have to help them understand why I've done the many things I've done. Because my work experience isn't linear and doesn't show a clear progression from one position to the next with gradually increasing responsibility and salary, I'm something of an enigma. I do my best to connect these dots in cover letters, but if hiring managers skip the cover letter and just read the résumé, I've got problems. I can make sense of it all in an interview, but to do that I've got to first get the interview.

While I'm proud of my experience, I'm also frustrated by it. As the job market has tightened up in the past few months, I've come to believe that the most important skills and experience in work and in life—communication, understanding, empathy, analysis, synthesis, and flexibility—are entirely transferable across jobs and industries, and it's diverse experience that builds these very skills. Technical skills and particulars can be learned on the job. When International Business Machines Corp. hired Lou Gerstner for its top job, he had no experience in the computer industry; it worked out OK for them. Just like Lou, I've moved from one interesting challenge to the next rather organically (layoff excepted) and across industry boundaries.

Have I "managed" my career? Not really. And perhaps I'm paying the price for not carefully constructing and managing a plan. I've spoken with people who've carefully constructed their careers. They envy my diverse experience and suspect I've had much more fun than they have. I sometimes think they're better off because it's easier for them to find a job, and they have a single-mindedness that I wonder whether I, at forty-one, should have. But I also love to just see what happens.

FIRST, NARROW THE FIELD

When Tim started job hunting, he found himself confronting a common career dilemma. He had held a variety of nonprofit and corporate jobs that, taken individually, had been stimulating and provided valuable experience. As a whole, however, his career path wasn't focused or cohesive. Add to that his M.B.A. degree, and the employers Tim contacted didn't seem to know where he might fit within their organizations.

To make matters more confusing, Tim himself didn't know what type of job he wanted to find. Calling himself a true generalist, his ideal was to locate a position that would use all of his skills, interests, and experience. In today's job market, though, employers seem uncomfortable with hiring generalists. Most of their openings are narrowly defined and they prefer to fit round pegs into round holes—in essence, to find specialists whose backgrounds exactly match the scope of the jobs they have open. And as long as it remains a buyer's employment market, employers have the luxury of being this choosy.

It's up to candidates, then, to turn themselves into round pegs that employers can "see" fitting into their holes. Yet many job seekers find themselves in the same situation as Tim. They start their careers on one track, only to decide they don't like it as much as they thought they would. Or an employer may ask them to take a role in a different functional area, so they start down a different path, giving their résumés a split personality. In a highly particular job market, job seekers lament that what should be a blessing—varied experience—becomes a curse.

I still don't know what I want to be when I grow up . . . Like Tim, I'm one of those early forty-somethings and my résumé confuses potential employers who want someone for a narrowly defined slot. —John C.

I am unfortunately in the very same situation—yet in many ways feel fortunate to have a broad vision and applied interest and ability. The world, on the other hand, seems to hate us, simply because we are sort of strange and hard to size up.—J.T.

This problem also presents itself in another way. As we age, we develop different interests and needs than we had as entry-level professionals. Those who are laid off after years in a traditional linear career path suddenly have a chance to think about whether they still like what they do. And for many, the answer is no. For them, the question becomes, "If not this, what?"

I am a fifty-year-old lawyer who has been in practice for ten years . . . I want to make a change, but I am not at all sure that I want to continue the rather stomach-churning practice of law. —Sharon A. Q.

I have been out of work since the end of June after twenty-four years in business development and sales. During the time with IBM, I was aware that I was performing a job for money and wasn t the least bit interested in the result (other than the cash!). After networking extensively, attending numerous interviews and, in general, pursuing jobs in the for-profit world, I have decided to pursue a career in lieu of pursuing a job. —Paul A.

WHAT IS "CAREER MANAGEMENT," REALLY?

Sharon and Paul are grappling with the relatively new concept of "career management." This hardly means signing on with a manager who will tell you what move to make next and arrange it for you in return for a fee, with the long-term goal of making you a star (although some talent managers do make money advising high-level executives this way). Or does it? In essence, this is exactly what's needed—but with *you* as the strategist, the talent, and the dealmaker .

Career management means having a long-term vision for yourself and making each move strategically instead of taking what's offered because it's easiest. As career managers, we become the shrewd directors of our own lives and refuse to put our fate in an employer's hands. We are opportunists who are highly self-interested in our own careers.

The concept of career management developed in the 1980s with the first wave of widespread white-collar layoffs. These spelled the end of the unofficial long-term contract between employers and employees—an unspoken agreement whereby companies would provide lifetime employment to employees who stayed to collect a gold watch at retirement. After their initial shock and disbelief subsided, laid-off employees realized that they needed to view themselves differently and to not put their trust in employers if they wanted to remain employable for the duration of their careers. The savviest among them began to remake themselves as portable "portfolio managers." Staying current in their function, remaking themselves to fit problems that needed to be solved, being highly flexible, and having loyalty to only themselves and their current assignments—these are the hallmarks of such managers.

As Tim continues writing his Diary, he begins to see himself this way. The following are some, but not necessarily all, of the qualities that distinguish good career managers:

- They have a life-plan. Good career managers have envisioned the type of life they want for themselves and their families and structured their careers to fit it. They know whether they want to live on a Colorado mountainside or near the Northeast Corridor, and they take steps to make that happen. They also are clear about how much free time they want and the type of work and format that will provide it to them.
- To create their life plan, they may be what Kurt Sandholtz, author of *Beyond Juggling: Rebalancing Your Busy Life* (Berrett Koehler Publishers Inc., 2002), calls "alternators" or "techflexers." Alternators "toggle between intensive focus on their work and intensive focus on nonwork life. For a period, they may throw themselves into their careers with abandon, then they may cut way back for a season and focus on their nonprofessional interests," says Mr. Sandholtz. Techflexers "leverage technology to the point that they can conduct their work from almost anywhere, any time. Not that they want to be working all the time. The key to this strategy isn't just technology but flexibility."

- These career self-managers know what they enjoy doing, and they direct their energies toward making it happen. Work isn't a burden for them. They aren't wrestling with what they want to be "when they grow up." The essential career self-searching is over for them—for now. They know their worth. This self-confidence and secure attitude make them attractive to employers and good negotiators for themselves.
- Career managers can envision the stepping-stones in their career path. They are aware of the skills and experience they need to collect to move them toward their goal. They are filling in the pieces necessary to complete their career jigsaw puzzles.
- They know that to reach the next step on the ladder, they need the recommendations that come from doing outstanding work, so their job performance is excellent. They concentrate on activities that will provide recognition and rewards.
- Career managers are excellent networkers. They are congenial lifelong buddies to others. Their networking is about what they can do for others because they know that what goes around comes around. They listen well and offer assistance or referrals whenever possible. If and when they are between jobs, they never have to struggle to find contacts who can provide advice and names of others they can call.

This posting to the Diary discussion board summed up some of these qualities:

Recently, I went to a speech where a CEO gave her testimony of her life. There were four important points she mentioned.

1. You never can communicate too much. Nobody can read our minds!
2. There is no secret in running your own business—just hard work, perseverance, and a little bit of luck.
3. Honor success, give back to the community, and keep dreaming.
4. Make sure your own life is in balance between work and personal life. "Nobody on their death bed ever said that they wished they had spent more time in the office." Remember, "Where I am today, I will not be tomorrow."

Keep pushing! —Keith T.

ASSESSING YOUR INTERESTS

Career management is neither a science nor a goal; rather, it's a lifelong effort. When we begin to see ourselves as people in process and realize that our journey is the destination, it becomes more of an adventure than an ordeal. But we'll be the first to admit it isn't easy. Nowadays, there are more jobs, professions, and industries than ever before.

"In 1850, the first U.S. census listed 322 job titles; in 2000, there were 31,000," writes reporter Cynthia Crossen in *The Wall Street Journal*. Social mores no longer dictate that we remain "organization" men and women who stay in the same path until we retire. We can take a step back, opt to become solo contributors instead of managers, start businesses, return to school, or explore life as independent consultants. As job hunters, we can seek the same type of position, stay in the same function but in another industry, or pursue three different roles simultaneously. We can work full- or part-time, telecommute, share jobs, or temp.

With so many career options available, who wouldn't want to crawl back under the covers or hire someone to tell us what to do?

For those wanting assistance, a variety of aids can be useful. In fact, an entire industry has developed over the past two decades to help people in transition answer the question: "What should I do next?" Career assessment and counseling is a multimillion-dollar business. Self-assessment testing usually is provided as part of outplacement counseling or by independent career counselors and university career centers. But while you can pay almost any amount for career assistance, you also can do it yourself at minimal expense using online quizzes and books.

If you have the time and ability to explore this question online, you might as well do it on the cheap. You always can pay to see a career professional later on. Many "Diary" readers told Tim they weren't happy with formal testing and encouraged others to use the homespun approach.

All of the career assessments told me what I already knew: that I enjoy being around people, public speaking, and writing. My suggestion is not to pay for any of these analyses. In lieu of this, figure out what your passion is and follow your heart. By the way, I did research, found articles about individuals who switched careers, and contacted several of them. One consistent theme is that they are all happier than before and none did a formal career assessment. They each pursued their own "yellow brick road."
—Paul A.

I've just been laid off from the only job I've had since I finished college eleven years ago (for a Big Five information-technology consultancy) . . . I've been taking tests and online self-assessments, but don't feel I'm much closer to identifying a type of work that would really turn me on (a recent self-assessment from a very reputable university pointed me to a list of careers that included television reporter, economist, and "jewelry/cosmetics generalist"). —Jon H.

A career counselor even wrote,

I have yet to find the one perfect assessment that will tell someone what they should do. People and work are frankly too complicated. I give a battery of assessments and from those develop themes and a context with which an individual can explore options. While a fascinating process, after ten years, I still think it's fairly complicated and not as simple as some would like. —Cathy S.

HELPFUL RESOURCES

Once you start dipping into the well of the Internet, you'll find an enormous number of online sites offering career aptitude tests and other self-assessment aides. To simplify your quest, consider using two helpful resources as guides to what we view as the "best of the best":

WHAT COLOR IS YOUR PARACHUTE?
BY RICHARD N. BOLLES (TEN SPEED PRESS, 2002).

This book provides tips to help you search for a job the right way for the rest of your life. It also offers tips to help you find your ideal job, starting with chapter 7, "The Secret to Finding Your Dream Job." This starts with envisioning the life you want and then finding work that supports this vision. What follows are a variety of methods to help the undecided job hunter narrow his or her choices. We particularly like Mr. Bolles's advice about career-assessment tests: (1) they aren't really tests, so you can't flunk them, and (2) treat the tests as suggestive only. Their main goal is to give you ideas you haven't thought of. If you expect them to tell you what to do with your life, you're expecting too much.

Visit Mr. Bolles's website, www.jobhuntersbible.com, in conjunction with perusing his book. It offers a list of useful tests and advice to be found on the Web. Mr. Bolles is generally complimentary about them: "With career counseling you enter a job-hunting arena where the Internet comes close to giving you what you'd hope for. True, the Internet still cannot replace the value of a live career counselor—even if the Internet does have email and chat rooms. But, so far as generic career counseling without a human body is concerned, you can indeed find much of what you'd hope to find on the Internet."

GUIDE TO INTERNET JOB SEARCHING, 2002-2003
BY MARGARET RILEY DIKEL AND FRANCES E. ROEHM,
PUBLIC LIBRARY ASSOCIATION (VGM CAREER BOOKS, 2002).

Ms. Dikel was among the first to recognize the power of the Internet for job seekers, and her book remains one of the best resources on job hunting and career resources available. It lists sites you can consult for career counseling, as does her continuously updated website, www.rileyguide.com. This is a virtual one-stop shopping portal for finding career tools and information on the Web. Enter her section entitled "Preparing for a Job Search" and you'll find descriptions of and links to more free, low-cost, and other fee-based career-assessment aids than you can possibly use.

STAYING WHERE YOU ARE

Perhaps this isn't the time to try something new. It's not unlikely that after all this self-assessing, you may decide you are already in your ideal job. Julie Jansen, a Stamford, Connecticut, coach and consultant, has identified six primary reasons why most people are dissatisfied with their current jobs. In her book, *I Don't Know What I Want, but I Know It's Not This: A Step-by-Step Guide to Finding Gratifying Work* (Penguin Books, 2003), she discusses the major sources of work-life situations that prompt changes in people's professional lives. They are:

- A desire for more meaningful work
- Bored, but still need a paycheck
- A downsizing or discrimination
- Boredom, in need of new challenges
- A desire for independence
- An approaching retirement

Think about why you want a change. Once you identify a root cause, you can gain a clearer understanding about the best steps for you to take next—whether it's to leave your current work situation and try something new or to make changes to add what may be missing in your current work situation.

MAKING MANY SKILLS FIT ONE OCCUPATION

Those with multiple skills shouldn't be discouraged. What career veteran hasn't developed a wide range of skills and abilities? Consider this missive from a job seeker:

I am a chartered accountant and have worked in all facets of the finance function for seventeen years in various multinational corporations. For the past four years, I have been working managing donor funds for the government in one underdeveloped country. I took up the job to add what I then thought was versatility to my CV. But now that my children are growing up and I want to move on to a developed country with a corporate job, I find no takers. The diverslty in my CV has led to naught in my search. —Subhasis S.

Be proud of your diverse skills and abilities. Now think strategically about them. Package them so that your focus seems narrower than you know it to be. (After you are hired, you can gradually let an employer know the true range of your abilities.) Or select the ones you enjoy using most—or that are most marketable—and exploit them. While some job hunters worry that they are fudging the truth, no deception is involved. You're stating the truth even if you rearrange the facts somewhat. There are several nuts-and-bolts techniques for presenting yourself this way in your résumé:

- Isolate and focus on one thread in your background
- Emphasize accomplishments and responsibilities that relate to a specific role you want (you may want to prepare several résumés emphasizing different roles)
- Group related jobs together at the start of your résumé, followed by those that deviated from your desired track
- Prepare a functional résumé that emphasizes your functional experience, followed by your job history (be mindful, however, that most hiring managers prefer chronological resumes; for more on chronological versus functional résumés, see chapter 3)

Taking courses or becoming certified, moonlighting, or volunteering in the field you most desire can also show your sincere commitment to one particular avenue.

You can take advantage of multiple and diverse skills and experience by seeking out employers who most value this type of background. Typically, these are small, growing, or otherwise less traditional organizations. (This also is a good strategy for older job hunters, who, not surprisingly, usually have varied experience and tend not to fit well into large bureaucratic companies.) Philadelphia career counselor Douglas B. Richardson describes such companies as "transformational." "They are more likely to put emphasis on what you can do, not what you are—or were, before that big downsizing," he says.

Again, the bottom line is your ability to make employers "see" you the way you want to be seen, says Mr. Richardson. "You must articulate to potential employers what you bring to the party," he says. "The successful rollout of any product requires the buyer to be able to perceive its features, benefits, and differentiators."

It also helps to realize that the world of work is dynamic and ever-changing. At the current fast pace of change, what an employer required yesterday is no longer the case today, says career author Tom Jackson. A job is outdated almost before it's filled, he says. What employers need is your ability to solve problems—your capabilities and ability to produce fresh results. In other words, this is an ideal time for a multiskilled person. "Mix and match skills, capabilities, values, interests, family, and environment," says Mr. Jackson. "Play with the pieces. Brainstorm fifty job possibilities that would fit the matches. Go after three or four of them at once."

THINKING OUTSIDE THE BOX FOR YOURSELF

Tim wasn't clear about how to narrow his options when he wrote this installment. As Francisco M. told the discussion group in an email:

Tim is shooting [in]to the air to see if he can [hit] something. In that way, things won't work. He needs to get a better idea of what he wants to do. Specifically, he should determine the type of work he wants to do and possible industries of interest, and he should research to find companies in the best shape to hire him.

When envisioning your options, why think in terms of what you've always done, in the way you've always done it? Some resourceful people are creating careers that combine several different jobs or are working part-time so they can develop other interests that may pay off down the road. Explore how to apply your abilities to employers' needs in a way that accomplishes your goals.

WORKING FOR YOURSELF

The shock of a layoff can be the push some people need to realize that they're responsible for their own destiny. You'll need to start thinking as if you are the president of Me, Inc. With the days of job security long gone, we're all self-employed, really. And some find fulfillment and satisfaction working for themselves, so they channel their passion into starting their own business.

To be sure, going solo as an entrepreneur isn't for everyone. But you still can think of yourself as a business that has customers, vendors, work processes, inventory (personal energy), income, and expenses. You'll need to start actively managing your career and evaluate decisions you make in terms of your overall career goals.

CONSULTING VERSUS CORPORATE

Tim mentions that if he were single, consulting would be a perfect career choice. Indeed, candidates with varied skills and corporate experience often think they can tie it all up neatly as consultants. And it's possible that with their years of experience they might fit some area of the consulting industry. It's important to note, however, that consulting firms rarely hire corporate executives as consultants unless they've been clients or fit a very particular need. Firms value prospective senior-level consultants and partners mostly for their rain-making ability; from their years of developing relationships, they can bring in lucrative clients—something most executives can't do.

Former executives who become consultants also must make a big practical change in how they work. At consulting firms, they become profit centers (hopefully) and bill clients by the hour. In essence, their billable hours justify their continued employment. Once they reach senior levels, consultants typically must generate their own client projects. They are simultaneously sales professionals, client-relations managers, and project leaders. Problem-solving—the so-called "fun" part—often takes up the smallest portion of their time. And Tim is right: most consultants work long hours and travel as much as 80 to 90 percent of the time.

I had the luck or misfortune to have to take a break (completely not job-related) from my consulting career at Accenture Ltd. in August 2001 (just before all this turmoil) and, well, my break is almost over and I am considering returning to the industry. However, I am not quite sure I'll be joining the same company or even the same industry altogether. The changes are

so many in the industry as a whole that I am having second thoughts about developing my career through consulting. You see, in the 1990s, consulting was where it was at as far as developing skills and acquiring relevant experience. Today, I feel that not only is it harder to join in, but the work done isn't as relevant. Am I completely wrong here? What would you say to somebody in my position? Would any of you go back? —Luis G.

Starting your own independent consulting business as a solution to your job-finding woes carries its own set of problems. Former executives think this may be the answer because they'll get to do what they're best at, minus the bureaucratic hassles. But unless you have at least one client to begin with, you will be consumed with finding work immediately. Most executives who make the transition say selling their services—especially without a track record—is the hardest, most unlikable aspect of their role. Further, in your first years of consulting you probably won't earn as much as you did in corporate America, yet you'll need to pay for your own benefits and do your own administrative work.

CONTRACT WORK

In 2002, about two million people were working on contracts or as temps in the United States, according to a survey by the American Staffing Association released in March 2003. This work mode blends consulting, part-time, and full-time formats in that most contract employees take fairly long-term assignments with companies. The primary distinction between contractors and full-timers (besides knowing that their stints will end) is that contractors aren't on the payroll and don't receive benefits.

As a contractor, you don't always have to find your next job yourself. Agencies and staffing firms abound to place qualified contractors in assignments. If you sign on with such a firm, you are likely to be on its payroll and possibly receive subsidized benefits, such as health insurance, or even paid vacation time. In effect, you are the agency's employee. The agency also assumes such employer tax responsibilities as paying into Social Security, worker's compensation, unemployment, and disability.

Some contractors and executive temporaries are highly paid, earning as much as or more than they did in their previous full-time roles. Those who qualify for top temp jobs have specific, highly valued skills, such as the ability to turn around a debt-ridden company, manage a department while a full-time employee is on a leave of absence, conduct an audit, or write software for a computer program.

Contractors are an independent lot; they usually relish the challenge of coming in to solve problems, enjoy being "outsiders" who are often asked to make tough decisions, and like the variety of working for many different companies. Contractors also enjoy being able to take off long periods of time to pursue their hobbies and interests. For example, one in-demand Seattle computer programmer works for about six months a year and travels by motorcycle to exotic countries during the remainder.

Working as a temp has often proved to be an effective job-search strategy. It is far easier to land a job at a company if you're already there in some capacity. You can talk to employees about openings, review job postings, and find out about new developments that might lead to opportunities with infinitely more ease and potential for success than you can as a jobless outsider. Employers are far more interested in hiring people they know and who have demonstrated their worth than they are in bringing in an unknown. If you are open about your desire to work at a company, chances are good that you may be considered for employment there.

OTHER ALTERNATIVES

If you're flexible and resourceful, you may be able to work for an employer in other nontraditional ways that address its needs and eventually lead to the type of job you want. For instance, if you can solve a problem, an employer may hire you to work part time at first. After proving your worth, you will likely be first in line for a full-time opening. Mothers returning from maternity leave (and some fathers) often prefer this type of arrangement so they can spend more time with their newborns. After their children start school, or even before, these parents can move into full-time roles.

Another new accommodation that often works well for parents of young children is job sharing: an arrangement in which two equally qualified employees split the responsibilities of a single position. Job seekers who learn that a half job-share is available might leverage their ability to work in this fashion into a job offer.

Telecommuting has become more popular and acceptable, especially for sales professionals and other employees who work independently or on the road. After creating virtual teams of professionals who work from home, some employers find they save money by closing offices that once housed these workers. Telecommuters still work hard, of course, and must accomplish set goals, but they relish the ability to sometimes choose how and when they work.

It's common now for employees to work a day or two a week from home. But to gain this privilege, they must be key contributors who have proven they are highly self-motivated. Some executives are able to negotiate a day or two per week during which they can telecommute from a home office. For them, the key to securing this arrangement is to ask for it up front, during the negotiation stage.

YOUR "ELEVATOR" SPEECH

"If you don't know where you're going, how will you know what road to take?" a Chicago outplacement executive often asks. It's essential to have completed your career assessments and know what you want to do before you contact employers. If you don't know what you want, they won't figure it out for you.

The "elevator" speech—so called because you should be able to deliver it during a short elevator ride—should flow from your career goal. Essentially, it's a brief description designed to help you respond to contacts who ask, "What do you do?" or similar questions, such as:

- What are you looking for?
- What are your goals now?
- Where are you applying?
- How would you fit in here?
- How can I help you?

When creating your elevator spiel, start with an "I" statement that describes what you do best (and presumably want to keep doing) professionally: "I am a marketing specialist who helps early- and mid-stage companies find their unique voice."

Follow this with a second sentence stating a significant accomplishment or experience. "I was so good at this, in fact, that I was promoted twice in the last five years at my last agency."

A third sentence could include a short-term goal: "Now I want to move to the corporate side and help a growing company achieve its vision mainly through branding and organic marketing techniques."

Your fourth sentence should focus on the type of help you want: "Can you give me the names of three people I could contact for more information about such opportunities?"

Two important rules: Keep it brief and informal, and don't sell yourself short. It's not inappropriate to use superlatives: saying I'm "the best brand expert in Boston," "a really effective leader," or "a technical whiz" isn't going too far. If you don't toot your own horn, who will?

As Sara C. told Tim:

I agree with all of those who are giving you advice to refine your pitch: say it like you believe it and make it something that actually means something.

It goes without saying, of course, that you must restate and repeat your elevator speech until it seems natural and unforced.

LISTEN TO YOUR HEART

If something doesn't feel right about your search, it probably isn't right. Employers are seeking enthusiasm and commitment in new hires; they can easily tell if you are sincere or merely "talking the talk." You may not spend a lifetime at your next company, but you should expect to like what you do. Only in this way will you find the hours and energy you spend working enjoyable and be able to give it your all.

● ● ●

Trust your gut. You will know instinctively if this is the time to try something new. The benefits of taking a new path will outweigh the negatives. Put another way, the negatives of staying in the same job or field will exceed the drawbacks of leaving it.

CHAPTER 3

WHY RÉSUMÉ REVISION MEANS NEVER BEING DONE

March 17

When I graduated from business school two years ago, I had a sparkling new résumé. It had been worked and reworked—by the school's career-placement office, my wife, friends, and trusted advisers.

The career office demanded final approval. When its writers were done, my essence had been distilled onto a single page—a page so dense I feared it would collapse under the sheer weight of the toner fused onto it. I dreaded gaining new experience, for it would force me to redo entirely what had taken hundreds of hours to create.

Getting laid off immediately ended the one- versus two-page résumé debate for me. I couldn't possibly incorporate my most recent experience without spilling onto a second page. At age forty-one, I have fifteen years of relevant experience, and I don't believe that a cogent history can fit on a single page. To start my search, I hastily updated my one-pager by adding my most recent job and increasing the white space and font size to make it a respectable two-pager. I sent it off in response to a dozen online postings, with no result. I figured I'd have to redo it once my family and I relocated to Princeton, New Jersey, from Boston. That redo is still underway . . . because a résumé is never done.

Without the b-school's placement office to assist me, I sought new counsel. And there's no shortage of it. Résumé advice is available from countless sources, both professional and personal. In fact, everyone's an expert.

I started with friends and family. I knew I had major work ahead when my father's only comment after reading it was, "So what?" Two years before, when I'd showed him my résumé, his response had been, "Wow, I'd like to hire that guy." I think his downsized response is a sign, not that my dad is becoming a curmudgeon, but of the times. Two years ago, I was a hot commodity on the job market—now I'm having a hard time getting my calls returned. I'm hoping that the two master's degrees I acquired in the interim haven't made me less attractive.

"AN AWFUL LOT OF WORK"

For help with my résumé makeover, I bought books on the subject. One says a good résumé is the key to opening doors. Another, which was actually a better read, explained that I should never send a résumé to anyone until after an interview.

This is where the dichotomy began. I'd have to live uncomfortably between these two camps—no résumé at all versus "résumé is all"—until I could create a vehicle for communicating my worth that made me feel comfortable. The résumé-is-all camp is split on the question of chronological or functional format. Only résumé professionals seem to like the functional format—everyone else tends to find it confusing.

I sought advice from two professionals in my network: a friend in the human-resources field and a career counselor. While their recommendations were completely contradictory, they both agreed that reading my résumé was "an awful lot of work."

And so the revisions resumed. I played with chronological and functional formats. I tried creating an objective, but everything I came up with was either too specific or too general.

Reading some general objectives can be a riot. I remember scanning them on candidates' résumés when I was hiring. They read something like this: "A challenging position that will utilize my skills and experience to create value for the company." What good is a statement like this? It implies that some other people would like unchallenging positions in which they don't create anything for anyone.

Specific objectives can be even funnier. Do employers really believe that it's kismet when a candidate's objective exactly matches the job description? "Hurray! We can all go home. We've found Mr. Right!"

It all boils down to creating a picture with the correct words, using as few of them as possible. What are the correct words? You can't reveal too much personality. Forget humor, because it might backfire. No group affiliations. Since prospective employers have their own particular tastes, the safe thing is to be entirely neutral. Plain vanilla. Does the vanilla candidate really ever get the job?

What about keywords? I read a frightening account of a company that takes a red pen and draws circles around words in an applicant's résumé that match words in the job description. The 10 percent of résumés with the most red circles make the first cut. An acquaintance recommended using hidden text to stuff every conceivable keyword into an online résumé. That makes a lot of sense to me. Using this technique, I can score a hit for every possible job in the world. Imagine the goodwill generated each time an employer views my résumé and sees that I have no actual qualifications for its job.

LOSING SLEEP

On several occasions, I have woken at night from a sound sleep, having had a vision of the perfect wording for a job-description bullet. "I didn't allocate, I formulated!" "I instituted, not initiated!"

By incorporating such visions—and distilling the advice of these many experts into a subset of what I hoped were higher truths—I reworked my accomplishments. I told myself that, thanks to word processing, I didn't have to destroy anything in order to experiment. I added an objective, a summary, and a list of applicable keywords. I removed the list of programming languages and software. I fleshed out my job bullets to identify a challenge, show how I solved it, quantify the results, and report the wondrous outcome ("Thus, the world was saved").

I flirted with a hybrid functional/chronological format. Then I showed it to my wife's stepmother. "Too many words," she said. She's a Ph.D. (My closest résumé advisers—my wife, her father, and her stepmother—are all Ph.D.s.) So, I eliminated bullets, leaving only the most tantalizing. When I was finally done, I barely recognized myself. Although an employer might instantly "know" who I was from the résumé, I no longer did.

I've since removed the objective, kept the summary and the keywords, restored many of the job bullets and the software list, and put the whole thing back into chronological order. I can cut many things, but removing jobs is like cutting away pieces of my soul. I think back to jobs that were displaced from my résumé long ago, and wonder how they're doing now. Did they find work on someone else's résumé? With great pain, I forced myself to remove two earlier jobs that were slightly out of line with my later experience. I removed them because they had completely stumped my HR friend when he'd inspected my résumé. "Whoa," he'd said. "Now I'm completely confused about who you are. You're making it very hard for me."

In the middle of this, I sent away for some sales materials from a résumé service. When they arrived, I found the marketing effort to be quite impressive. The package included a CD with multimedia testimonials. Some of the service's satisfied customers apparently have received multiple offers overnight at salaries two to three times higher than what they previously made. Then I looked at the enclosed résumé samples. I thought they looked tacky and contained lots of puffery. I know someone who paid $4,000 to have her résumé done professionally, and it still looks like crap. But, what do I know? Still, I'm suspicious when someone proclaims that he's "dynamic."

So I now have a résumé that I sort of like. But since I understand that I'm supposed to tailor my résumé for each job application, I already have dozens of permutations. As soon as I get a job, I'm going to hire a staff to keep them organized.

GIVEN ALL THE CONFLICTING ADVICE ABOUT RÉSUMÉS, WHAT'S THE BEST APPROACH?

As Tim starts to gear up his search efforts, he hits on one of the most anxiety-inducing components of job hunting: preparing an effective résumé. Your résumé is a critical document—it can make or break your candidacy—and it's one piece of your search over which you actually have complete control. For many candidates, that means the seemingly endless rounds of revisions will become the most time-consuming aspect of your search at this stage

Tim's experience strikes a nerve—he expresses a frustration universally felt by job seekers. Consider some of the responses job seekers posted to his discussion board:

I had my résumé professionally written and rewritten. I get conflicting feedback on the length, format, and information included from various consultants and recruiters. But I know one thing: It isn't working well enough to get me where I want to go. Interviews are few and far between. —Mike K.

I am in a real quandary and find myself reaching a very desperate point. I am tired, feel beat-up, and really don't know what to do next. I have had my résumé done professionally, and I have written ten iterations of it myself. Each cover letter is carefully 'wordsmithed' to meet the needs of the opportunity. I check and double-check, only to have nothing happen.—LJ

When your search isn't yielding results, your résumé becomes an easy target. And outplacement counselors report that for some professionals, the revisions can border on obsession, to the point where they become counterproductive. The busywork of revision becomes a way to procrastinate—you feel as if you're doing something, but all you're actually doing is spinning your wheels.

Of course, your résumé may really deserve the blame. Unless you're fortunate enough to know the hiring manager personally or to have arranged an introduction through networking, the résumé is usually the deciding factor in getting you an interview or, conversely, sending your candidacy to the circular file (which, given the Internet, is usually a virtual one nowadays). If you have revised your résumé numerous times and you still aren't getting interview invitations, consider asking a respected friend or professional for an objective opinion about whether to do more rewriting.

There's no doubt that a powerful presentation can make a difference. And although the improvements you make may not seem that significant, they may somehow help you connect more effectively with hiring managers. As this job seeker reported:

After months of nothing at all, suddenly I've been called in for an interview (and made the cut for round two), scheduled another, and had five inquiries from prospective employers. All of this has transpired over the past four days. Only one has been a direct-employee offering, but after a long time, anything is an improvement. Yeah! The telephone is ringing, and it's not a bill collector! The only thing I can attribute this reversal of fortunes to is a subtle change in my résumé presentation and a recent dramatic change in my opening pitch/cover letter. —Arne B.

EXPERTS DISAGREE ON THE BASICS

Making the task of résumé-writing even more puzzling, professional résumé writers are often at odds on the best tactics and techniques. As Tim points out, one camp of experts says to never use a two-page résumé; another says that for most executives, a two-page résumé is best. One group says the only way to organize a résumé is chronologically; another says arranging your experience by function is just fine. Don't even bother asking more than one résumé professional about the value of including an objective at the top of your document. You'll likely get two different answers.

Even career coaches and professional résumé writers acknowledge the confusion. As one professional told the online discussion group:

You've discovered the absolute lack of consensus among careers-industry authors and professionals as to what works and doesn't work in contemporary job-search and career management. —Deborah W.D.

With all this conflicting advice, how do you determine your best approach? One point on which most career counselors and professional résumé writers do agree is that you'll need more than one version of your résumé. "One size fits all" doesn't cut it in today's complex job market.

The only thing I found that works is to 'mold' your résumé to emphasize your talents that fit the specific job. Don't lie, but simply show that your skills are applicable. It means a different résumé for every job, but it can work. —Peter J.

Despite optical scanners and high-tech résumé-storage databases, busy human-resources managers don't have the time to peruse your document and apply their best out-of-the box-thinking skills: "This applicant doesn't fit our specs, but I have a hunch he'll be a perfect match anyway! Call him immediately!" Hoping for this kind of reaction is, alas, pure fantasy. So before you get down to writing your self-marketing masterpiece, consider the following advice on length and format.

THE ONE-PAGE VERSUS TWO-PAGE DEBATE

- "Hiring managers are so busy, they look only at one-page résumés."
- "Experienced job hunters need two pages to describe all their accomplishments."

Have you heard the one-page/two-page résumé debate before? Unfortunately, there's no right answer—but for certain purposes, one length is more effective than the other.

The main argument for the one-page-only résumé is that time is money. Your résumé is effective only if it leads to interviews. You have, at most, thirty seconds to convince a prospective employer that your background warrants attention. If your résumé is well written, it should summarize the qualifications and experience most likely to interest the employer you're targeting. With creativity and a sharp pencil, the average two-page résumé can be condensed into a targeted, tightly constructed one-page document.

Résumés were never intended to include everything you've accomplished in your career. Few employers—at least at the résumé stage—are concerned with what you did in your early professional life. The second page of a résumé typically describes first jobs, educational credentials and military service, and additional skills or training. Some of this information is ancient history and needn't be included.

Many candidates should heed this advice. For some, however, there are compelling arguments for a two-page document. To begin with, you may not be able to squeeze your qualifications into one page—and if you try, your résumé may end up looking like a cookie-cutter duplicate of all the others stacked on a hiring manager's desk. It may do little more than simply list your experience in small type, much like a list of ingredients on a can of food. Readability can be a concern.

Most job seekers who joined Tim's discussion came down firmly in the two-page résumé camp. A sample:

Condensing all of your best attributes into one page is a challenge for the applicant and certainly doesn't give the interviewer enough data to make a decision to request the first interview. —Lewis P.

Further, your résumé is likely to be scanned into a massive résumé database that companies can search electronically for potential candidates. That's when having plenty of "keywords" comes in handy. Typically, the selection software program hunts for résumés containing these words or phrases describing certain job or applicant requirements. If your résumé is too brief to include enough keywords describing what you can do, the selection software won't pull it out of the hordes for jobs you just might be suited for. Be sure to keep them relevant to your candidacy, or you'll risk alienating hiring managers.

There are other circumstances in which a longer résumé is appropriate. Candidates in fields such as academia, medicine, or science may require up to six pages or more. Similarly, senior executives with extensive backgrounds may fare better with a two- or even a three-page document. Each situation requires a different strategy. When writing your résumé, consider your background and situation. You can even send in a shorter version to snare an interview, then bring along a longer version to the meeting, as this job seeker suggested:

For executives and technical people, have two résumés: one short and one long. The short one is for marketing and the second one is for detailed discussion. Common notions of length are nonsense. You can write a résumé from one to a hundred pages. Do what works and what's best. There's no law here. A résumé is for marketing and communications. —Joe

ONLINE RÉSUMÉS

Some professionals find a solution to the page-length dilemma by using an online résumé in conjunction with a conventional résumé. Here are two strategies from job seekers and the advice they gleaned from their experiences:

By providing a path from a general to the online résumé, the reviewer can drill down to detail in any specific area. (The obvious downside is that one would already have to be very interested in order to pursue the online version.) I see this perhaps working best as a URL on a personally delivered business card, where it might not be competing with the flood of résumés that follows an ad. Think of it as the refrigerator-magnet concept.
—Day C.P.

For an IT professional, an online résumé only makes sense (at least for now), but I think anyone with basic desktop-publishing skills can create one and host it with many free hosting providers. First, I lure hiring managers in by creating a cover letter and sending them my standard résumé, both documents encouraging them to come to my website for further information (cover letters, personal abstract, skills inventory, etc.). Next, I sit back and watch my logs to see who actually came to the website, which pages they chose to look at, how much time they spent looking at each page, etc. I know which companies came to my site and [I] send a personal email, thanking them for coming and elaborating on the subject material contained within the pages they viewed the longest. If I see a page that doesn't get much attention, I modify and reformat the information to get a better response. —Jim P.

CHRONOLOGICAL OR FUNCTIONAL FORMAT

When it comes to choosing the format of your résumé—chronological or functional—for most people, the choice is easy: Recruiters in corporate human-resources departments usually prefer to see employment histories in reverse chronological order. They like to see a progression of learning and responsibility and a logical sequence to your career moves. Career counselors and professional résumé writers usually recommend using this format if at all possible.

In a tight job market, résumé screeners are usually overwhelmed with applications and are looking for easy reasons to disqualify candidates so they can whittle down the stack of résumés on their desks. This job seeker laid out another reason why it's a good idea to stick with a chronological format:

Hiring managers are curious about a candidate's history. If you do it functionally, they get confused, their gut says something is wrong, and they pass on the résumé. —Logan F.

Still, if you're changing careers or have held a portfolio of varied jobs, you might be better off creating a functional résumé. This format starts by summarizing your most significant skills and accomplishments rather than listing a work history. A functionally formatted résumé focuses attention on what you've done that relates to the position you're seeking, not where you've worked or your past job titles. As such, it helps make a case for why you should be considered for a job, even if you haven't held similar positions in the past. Both chronological and functional formats offer advantages depending on your circumstances. Select the appropriate one for your needs.

INCLUDE AN OBJECTIVE: YES OR NO?

Whether to include an objective on your résumé is a judgment call. Some experts recommend doing so because it helps résumé readers to know exactly what type of job you're seeking. If you're applying for a particular vacancy, writing an objective that dovetails with the description of the opening—without *exactly* copying it—can be a nice touch and shows you have a strong desire for the role. Otherwise, unless you're new to the job market or are changing careers, an objective is not really needed. It's also possible that if your objective is too narrow or significantly different in other ways from what a hiring manager has in mind, it could backfire—and knock your résumé out of the running.

Cut the objective unless you need to explain what you are looking for. Too often it's bland stuff like "a challenging position that will enable me to use my skills and experience." Go right to your career history. —John N.

THE COMMONSENSE APPROACH

Once you've decided on the basics of length and format, it's time to get down to the business of deciding what to include and what to leave out of your résumé. Reviewing your career history to construct a résumé can be a daunting task. Career experts advise job hunters to analyze their backgrounds carefully to select the material that best meets the needs of a target employer. Your career may be full of impressive results, but the business world measures success by what you've done lately. Your document should emphasize recent achievements, higher-level functions, and experience most relevant to your goal—and the position the employer is offering.

With résumés, as with most things in life, taking a commonsense approach usually works best. Before you send off your résumé, ask yourself a final question: if you were the hiring manager, would you call yourself for an interview? Many participating on the discussion board advised forgetting the so-called rules. "Make it a good read," wrote Deb W. D., the professional résumé writer. Several readers offered their own résumé litmus tests:

I also had all sorts of "experts" tell me what should or shouldn't be in a résumé, so I eventually ended up with a résumé that has information that I would look for if I were hiring somebody. —Dennis S.

Think of the résumé as a direct-response mail piece or late-night infomercial—"Pick up the phone right now, operators are standing by!" The point is to pique [readers'] curiosity enough for them to call you in for an interview. If you tell them too much up front, the thrill is gone. They pigeonhole you based on a piece of paper. Keep it simple, factual, and tantalizing. —Logan F.

A career coach shared his formula for appraising a résumé:

1. Does it look good?
2. Does it read well?
3. Does it describe who I am, what I've done and—most important— what I'm capable of doing?

Forget résumé advice from human-resources folks, recruiters and most career counselors. The best advice will come from hiring managers. At your level, that's where your résumé should be ending up initially. If a recruiter wishes to reformat your résumé for a particular client, that's fine, but that version shouldn't become your new résumé. Avoid HR—they hire only HR people. —Bill S.

NO JOB FOR AN AMATEUR?

Once you have a résumé that you're happy with, it's always advisable to get second, third, or more opinions on it. Colleagues, references, recruiters, and even hiring managers are a great source of feedback. Members of job-search support groups usually are willing to provide informal résumé feedback to one another. Colleges and professional schools are another source of free, or nearly free, résumé guidance.

For the truly "résumé challenged," paying a professional résumé writer may be a worthwhile expense. It can be a relief to hand over the task to someone else, especially if you aren't sure that you've done it "right." And professional help can be especially important for candidates with specific challenges, such as an extended period without work.

One of the pitfalls of using a professional résumé writer is that your document can end up sounding like other candidates'—or worse yet, it may not sound like you. Another downside is overwriting: your document may end up loaded with empty phrases such as "results-focused" and "detail-oriented." And remember, even if someone else is helping you, you'll need to do the bulk of the work.

There are hundreds, perhaps thousands, of résumé writers nationwide. Just about anyone can hang out a shingle as a professional résumé writer, so ask for references. A good résumé writer certainly doesn't need certification, but some have sought accreditation from professional résumé writers' organizations. Here are the three largest groups in the United States:

- Professional Association of Résumé Writers & Career Coaches
- National Résumé Writers' Association
- Professional Résumé Writing and Research Association

Even though you can check for certifications and ask for references, the quality of professional résumé writers can vary widely. Consider the experience of this public-relations professional who wrote in to Tim's discussion board:

I decided to upgrade my résumé to reflect more results and management experience and went to a professional résumé writer. But after writing fifteen pages of my detailed experience, she spit it out in the exact same verbiage I had given her. Plus, when she wanted me to sit with her and rewrite it, I knew I was getting snowed. I told her that I can't edit and review things this quickly. I took it home, worked on it myself, and requested a refund. I'm still waiting for it.

I also went to a consultant to whom I paid an hourly fee. He gave me some insight about writing my experience and accomplishments in detail. He also gave me good advice about pulling the keywords from the job posting and using them when I write a cover letter. —Debra S.

RÉSUMÉ BLASTERS

In addition to outsourcing the writing of a résumé, job seekers today can automate its distribution. A résumé-blasting service can send your document to thousands of hiring managers over the Internet for a fee. But should you mass-email your résumé? While you may annoy those folks who see emailed résumés as little more than "spam," the expense and potential offensiveness is worth it if you connect with a single hiring manager who's looking for someone with your qualifications. The cost of mass-emailing a résumé starts at around $40 or $50. When selecting a service, choose one from which recruiters or human-resource managers opt in to receive mailings and that can target specific industries or regions. Otherwise, you may be wasting your time and money.

If you opt for this route and the service you hire isn't using a quality list, prepare for in-box overload, as job seeker Gary S. reports:

I paid a small fee ($50 or something) to spread my résumé across the Internet. Results included

- A mailbox full of cookie-cutter rejection cards and letters from companies I've never heard of—let alone in my industry or career field
- Solicitations to "help me build my résumé and contact the decision makers"—all for a fee from $5,000 to $15,000
- Solicitations to enter into a 100 percent commission financial-sales career.

Of course, this "lotto" approach to job searching may not be your style. Still, there's something to be said for favoring quantity over quality. At the start of his job search, each résumé and application Tim sent represented a time-intensive effort of research and polishing. But ultimately he concluded it was a numbers game. This job seeker who wrote in to his discussion board agreed, as did several others:

I have come to believe that quantity presently has the edge—just because of the sheer number of applicants on the market and the small number of openings. —Alfredo C.

A TARGETED JOB SEARCH

If you aren't getting responses from résumés you've sent in reply to ads, you're not alone. Job hunters shouldn't only respond to employment ads. Only a small percentage of jobs are advertised. Even with all the Internet services for job seekers, networking is still the most effective job-search tool.

This doesn't mean that when you see a posting for the perfect job, you should pass up the opportunity. Respond to it, but use a targeted approach. Reply only to those ads that list the name of an employer and contact person. Read the ad carefully and customize your résumé so that it's clear that you meet or exceed the requirements.

Research the organization to the extent that you can and tailor the first paragraph of your cover letter to the company and your specific interest in it. Using an individual's name in a cover letter is a much better way to start than, "To Whom It May Concern." Many readers wrote in about the necessity of networking—both pro and con—and making direct contact with employers:

I got the most response mailing my CV directly to the chief executive officer or to a managing partner. After all, they are the decision-makers. —Kelly T.

I found that, even when companies demanded "no phone calls," a call was still the best way to get a résumé in front of someone. Networking was completely fruitless, since nearly everyone I contacted also had no job. Nothing worked. I remember thinking, after September 11, "The whole world is going to hell and still nobody needs my help!" Here is what ulti-mately worked: the back door. I was working for a few customers of my own as an independent consultant and I needed services. I called a few compa-nies, not trying to sell myself, but looking to use their services. Once they considered me a sales lead, I could call or meet anyone I wanted. It wasn't long before I heard, "Do you have a résumé?"—Agmos

Bypassing the "gatekeepers" in the human-resources department is often a necessity. And it remains a challenge for job seekers:

How in the world do you bypass human resources and get the attention of a manager? I have been job hunting for almost seven months and I would say that out of every hundred contacts I've made, I have actually spoken to managers with hiring authority about five times. Without actually knowing somebody in the company, speaking to a manager is nearly impossible. —Tom G.

Indeed, these gatekeepers are jealous guardians of their turf. And, sure enough, one even wrote in to discourage folks from trying to bypass HR:

I am a "gatekeeper"—the head of human resources for a professional sports team. Bypassing HR is nearly impossible, but people try it every day, and every day our management team forwards résumés to my department that arrived on their desks from people that retrieved their names through various means. The hard truth is that candidates see our managers only once we have screened them as viable candidates and passed them on with our "HR blessings." This is the most common practice throughout many organizations. —Vivian L.

Undaunted, jobseekers nonetheless sent the discussion board road-tested tips and advice for storming the gates:

It is tough to bypass human resources, but it can be done. One idea is to attend and participate in conferences related to your specialty. You can frequently make contact with key people in the field over coffee or lunch. —John N.

If your company is a public entity, you could make a name for yourself by using the U.S. Securities and Exchange Commission's Edgar database (www.sec.gov/edgar.shtml) and looking at the latest 10K or 10Q reports. Find a name you like on the listings of corporate officers and/or directors. Send a nice cover letter asking him or her to forward your CV to the appropriate officer who heads your prospective department. I always get an acknowledgment—usually a call back. —Herb K.

You might try using the website for the company (if a search doesn't reveal the company's web address, try using the latter part of the email address—frequently it offers clues as to who the person is you're sending your info to). For example, bsmith@company.com may be revealed to be Robert Smith, vice president of sales. In addition, it could even work for human-resources contacts. You may find that hr@company.com is Ellen Roberts. You can at least address your cover letter to her.

If you're unsuccessful at ferreting out the info, then by all means send your résumé to "Hiring Manager." I do it all the time if I'm unable to find out a name. It also solves the gender issue. Sure it's impersonal, but if they don't want you to know who they are, it's their problem if they take offense at reading cover letter after cover letter addressed to "Dear Sir or Madam" or "Dear Human-Resources Director," etc. —Jeff A.

THE ROLE OF COVER LETTERS

Always include a cover letter, even if you're emailing your résumé. While some recruiters don't read them, others won't look at a résumé unless the cover letter tells them something compelling about a candidate. When you sit down to craft your letter, write the way you speak, and avoid gimmicks. The letter should give readers a sense of your personality and a reason why they should want to meet you, touching on your qualifications and your spirit. Show that you understand the employer's current issues: describe how your skills, expertise, and past accomplishments can help, going by the specifics of the job ad. Put yourself in the employer's place and think about what you'd like to hear from a candidate. For instance, you might cite a problem you know the company is having and how hiring you can help to resolve it.

A cover letter should showcase things that aren't in a résumé, so don't try to recap it. Mention how you learned about the opportunity at the company and why you're interested in it. It's OK to drop the name of someone you know at the company if this acquaintance can help you get a foot in the door. Be sure to first get their permission to use their name, however. When you're done, ask a friend or family member to give your letter a critical review. (For more advice on writing cover letters, see chapters 10 and 11.)

A FINAL WORD ON RÉSUMÉS

Whether you write and send your résumé yourself or seek help from the pros, make sure this key document is working as effectively as possible for you. Conducting a job search is like marketing and selling a product: you. Your résumé strategy can help boost your chances of landing interviews and the job you want. Remember, in every situation, you have options. If the tack you've taken isn't working, you don't have to languish in job-search limbo. Try another avenue.

● ● ●

An added benefit of writing a résumé is that it forces you to review everything you know about yourself. A winning résumé grabs the reader's attention and increases your chances of being called in for an interview. The rest is up to you.

CHAPTER 4

WHAT GETS RESULTS WHEN JOB HUNTING ONLINE

April 4

This week I got my first nibble in my job search. Three of them, actually, all within a three-hour period, three months after being laid off. Three interviews. I could barely catch my breath. Perhaps my luck is changing. What did I do that caused these three prospective employers to respond? If I can find a pattern, perhaps I can replicate it, and the world will start calling me. Could it be the result of posting my résumé on the right job site?

It's easy to look for jobs on the Internet. From the safety of the dining room, I can hunt for openings on any of the estimated forty thousand job sites and never have to interact with a human being. Because there are so many sites, looking for a job online can become a life's work. Fortunately, not all job sites are created equal. Here are a few tips on how to weed out the duds.

The two biggest sites are Monster and Hotjobs. I've posted my résumé on each of these and look for new listings daily. But forget the notion that just posting your résumé on a big site will lead to anything. Monster, for example, boasts fifteen million résumés in its active database. How many résumés pop up each time an employer runs a search? What are the odds that the right person will see your résumé? It's more likely that Babe Ruth will recapture the record for single-season home runs.

HANDY TIP: DIVERSIFY YOUR JOB-SEARCH METHODS, OR YOU'LL NEVER WORK AGAIN.

I reasoned that having a presence on smaller, more specific sites might increase the odds that someone would someday find me; I could use technology to do some of the heavy lifting for me. I looked for sites that specialize in M.B.A.s. MBAjobs.net comes out near the very top in most search engines, and is, by its own admission, the "world's foremost specialist forum for M.B.A.s." While it lists only four jobs in the entire United States, job seekers can use the employer features, free of charge, to find other M.B.A.s ready and willing to work in any country in the world. I selected "Vatican City" from the pull-down menu. No M.B.A.s there.

Another great thing about this site is that you don't have to worry about cutting and pasting your résumé—it doesn't accept them. Employers know only where you live and where you got your M.B.A. Unless you went to Harvard, don't wait by the phone.

HANDY TIP: AVOID SITES WITH NO JOBS AND THOSE WHERE THE INFORMATION YOU PROVIDE ABOUT YOURSELF IS TOO BRIEF TO BE OF USE TO AN EMPLOYER.

Many job sites seem to be dying a slow, painful dot-com death. I arrived on the home page of one such site and entered my search criteria. No jobs were found. After several progressively broader iterations, I created a search that would return every job posted on the site—all one of them, as it turned out. It was a position posted in 1999 for a registered nurse in Plano, Texas. Fascinated, I sent the webmaster an email, hoping to learn why or how the site continued to exist. No response. Perhaps the site had prepaid for ten years of hosting before it went bust.

Many other sites have jobs from a single employer. At Myjobsearch.com, I found all sorts of jobs—which was great as long as I wanted to work at a McDonald's unit in southern Utah.

HANDY TIP: AVOID SITES WITH JOBS POSTED BEFORE YOU WERE BORN AND THOSE WITH NO EMPLOYERS.

Other sites have plenty of jobs, but they all seem to be from the same five companies. This is fine if they're companies you want to work for.

HANDY TIP: REVIEW THE LIST OF COMPANIES THAT USE THE SITE BEFORE YOU BOTHER TO REGISTER, LOOK FOR JOBS, OR ADD IT TO YOUR LIST OF SITES TO CHECK DAILY.

Then there's the issue of intermediaries: recruiters, agencies, call them what you will. Now that jobs are hard to come by, recruiters seem more afraid than ever of being bypassed. I see the same job posted by multiple recruiters on multiple job sites; some of the details are changed, which makes it more confusing. One recruiter called me with "a program-manager position in Philadelphia." We've since been through four rounds of email and voicemail tag, and I still don't know anything about the job. Some recruiters also call themselves consultants. A search for jobs in the consulting industry on Vault.com yields a mixed bag of postings—from temp positions to construction jobs—because the agency that posted them said its industry is human-resources consulting.

The only people who have actually contacted me because they saw my résumé posted online are recruiters with leads that go nowhere, people trying to sell me something, and Amway-style multilevel-marketing financial-services sweatshops that want me to join forty other people at a seminar to hear about a great opportunity with unlimited growth potential.

Wonderful recruiters exist in this world; some are even friends of mine. I'm just not sure they're trolling for people on job sites.

HANDY TIP: THE BEST RECRUITERS DON'T HUNT FOR CANDIDATES ON THE INTERNET. DON'T WASTE YOUR TIME WITH THE TROLLS. IF THEY INDEED HAD A GOOD OPPORTUNITY, THEY WOULDN'T BE CALLING YOU.

So how did I get the three interviews?

Interview 1 is with a consulting firm looking for a marketing manager. I actually found this company by reading articles on a consulting website. After following a bunch of links, I stumbled onto the site. It wasn't advertising any jobs. The company intrigued me, so I mailed a letter and résumé to the head of recruiting, then I called and left a follow-up message, and he later called me back.

Interview 2 is with a publishing company looking for someone to create content for educational programs. I responded to a print ad that my wife came across in *The New York Times.* The only contact information the ad provided was a post-office box. I used the Internet to track down the phone number for the company, called and tried to get a name of a contact with no luck, and ended up sending a résumé to my old friend, Dear Sir or Madam. The chief executive officer called me about ten minutes after I got off the phone with the head of recruiting for Interview 1.

Interview 3 is with an advertising agency. It actually had an opening posted on a job site, but it wasn't right for me. I went to the company's site, got the president's name, and sent him a letter. His head of human resources sent me an email asking me to call him about a different position ASAP.

Only one of the three nibbles had any connection to a job site.

The Internet is great for research, but I'm learning to limit and focus the time I spend online. When I had my own consulting business, I loved the convenience of working from my home office in my bathrobe. Some days I wouldn't get dressed until noon. Now that I'm unemployed, sitting around in

COMPUTERS MAKE IT SEEM EASY

Too easy. That's the Internet's seduction for job seekers. Given how frustrating it is to search for jobs online, why do we spend so much time trolling for job listings, registering our résumé on job sites, emailing letters to employers, and mass-mailing recruiters? Tim's conclusions about the siren call of the Internet rang true to job seekers:

Using the Internet these days is like using blind newspaper ads—worthless!!! —P. Miller.

The ease with which I can send a résumé/cover letter over the Internet also means thousands of others can do the same. I've talked to both managers and recruiters faced with the avalanche of electronic credentials and to my horror, many admit to often throwing out entire stacks of résumés and resorting to networking. —Craig K.

Naturally, the more people who use the Internet to look for and apply for jobs, the more competition there is. Richard Bolles, author of *What Color Is Your Parachute?*, periodically estimates the odds that job seekers will be successful using the Internet to find work. With about sixteen million résumés floating in cyberspace and, by some counts, more than a hundred thousand job-related sites to visit, he judges the effectiveness of using the Internet to find a job at 4 percent.

A survey by CareerJournal.com and the Society for Human Resource Management indicates that almost all job hunters surveyed (96 percent) use the Internet as a job-search technique, but less than half (48 percent) say it's effective for them. About 90 percent complete online or website job applications, but this tactic is effective for only 36 percent of them. (Bear in mind that the questionnaire was emailed to Internet users, so the percentage of respondents employing the Web in their job search may be higher than that in the general population.)

I realize the Web is useless as a resource, one which I spend at least four to five hours with daily despite the facts. Sadly, it occurred to me: I've never gotten a job offer from the Web, and I've been around. —BKN

WHY IS CYBERSPACE SO APPEALING?

So why do job seekers seem to prefer sitting in the neon glow of a computer screen when clearly it's not the best use of their time?

- It seems effective. Being busy is seductive. If you're reading about actual jobs and updating and mailing your résumé, you feel as though you're accomplishing more than you really are.
- The Web is a great place to "get lost" and forget your unemployment woes, especially if you often take "side trips" to ancillary sites (and who doesn't?).
- Many of us are introverts at heart. We don't like having to sell ourselves, cold-call strangers, or ask networking contacts for help. It's infinitely preferable to do busywork than to call contacts personally. Dan N. described this syndrome to the Diary discussion group:

I agree you can spend too much time on the Internet sites. The downside of the Internet is that there is no human contact; you spend all day applying for jobs and really have not done anything at all to get that next job.

HOW MUCH TIME SHOULD YOU SPEND?

So you won't get caught in this trap, make a commitment to yourself to spend no more than 25 percent of your dedicated job-search time online, advises online job-search expert Margaret Riley Dikel. She bumps up the online time allotment to 50 percent if you're "a techie who is working in any area related to computer networks or programming." As for the rest of your time, spend a large portion networking and getting out to meet people. Mike, a participant in the Diary discussion, agrees:

The Internet is a complete waste of time, other than for information gathering. A few of you may have been successful with the job sites but not me. An article in *The New York Times* on the Internet as a search-and-application vehicle was quite eye-opening. It actually is a detriment to job hunting in some respects. As applying is essentially costless, everyone applies for everything. On occasion, thousands of résumés pour in on a single job. Your odds aren't good. The recommendation of the article: Spend no more than 20 percent of your job search on the Internet. I spent way too much time, partly because it is painless. But the lack of pain is essentially why it doesn't work.

GOING ONLINE CAN LEAD TO NEW CONTACTS

Nevertheless, no one disputes that cyberspace has a place in almost everyone's job search. To make their online time effective, like Tim, job hunters need to recognize the Internet's fallibilities and harness its power. One of its best features for job hunters is the many free or low-cost assessment aids that can help you to narrow your career choices. (See chapter 2.)

The Internet also can help you to network more effectively, and networking is a more likely avenue to a new job. Among readers of this Diary installment, the importance of networking was the most prevalent sentiment:

Applying for positions online is about as successful as taking your résumé and throwing it into a hurricane and hoping it gets to the 'right' person. Networking is the only way to go. —DD

Network, network, network. Let everyone know—no matter how dusty the Rolodex or email address list—that you're available. I don't think it matters how close you are to the recipient. If you had any business or personal interaction with them in the past, give it a shot. The worst that happens is nothing. The best is a hot lead. You have nothing to lose in using this strategy. —Arne B.

Tim, you are right, the best candidates come from traditional methods of recruiting: good ol' social/business networking. —vb

USING THE INTERNET TO NETWORK

Although you may find it difficult personally, talking with as many people as possible—asking them for information and advice and to remember you if they hear anything—is the best use of your time. The goal of networking is to meet people in a position to hire you and make a favorable impression on them. The payoff may not be immediate, but if you have enough of these encounters, sooner or later you will see results.

You can use the Internet to make your personal networking more effective by tapping its wealth of information to find people and learn about companies.

FINDING PEOPLE

Who hasn't exhausted their list of personal contacts within a few weeks of starting to job hunt? What then? How can we find names of others to call? This is where the Internet shines. If you're given the name of someone to contact, but no other information, you likely can find that person via the various websites designed to locate names, postal addresses, phone numbers, and email listings. You can also track down old friends, alumni, or former colleagues. Sites that can help you do this include Yahoo! Inc.'s PeopleSearch (http://people.yahoo.com) and Addresses.com (www.addresses.com).

As Tim did, you can find names of new networking contacts by reading articles about your field or industry on news magazine and association websites. (This tactic led Tim to an interview invitation.) You can seek names of executives in particular functional areas on many corporate directory or company websites.

LEARNING ABOUT COMPANIES

No one likes to talk with an uninformed job seeker. Don't even think about calling networking contacts or hiring managers until you know pertinent facts about the companies they work for and those you're targeting. Explore company websites; review business-directory sites to learn about industry trends, the company and its competitors; read articles on magazine websites; or type the firm's name into www.google.com and see what pops up. You also might want to visit the U.S. Securities and Exchange Commission's EDGAR online database (www.sec.gov/edgar.shtml) for corporate filings required by law. For more on doing your homework on employers, see chapter 6.

SEEKING COMMUNITY ONLINE

The Internet allows us to create "community"—to form relationships with like-minded people—in ways we never could before. Speaking with other job hunters and knowing that they have the same feelings as you can help you beat the blues and isolation of searching by yourself. The Diary discussion group is testimony to the power of this concept. It's obvious that a bond developed among participants. Many sought advice from and offered it to each other, and some exchanged email addresses to stay in touch.

Through professional associations, executive membership organizations, alumni groups, fraternal organizations—the possibilities are endless—you can meet others who can provide support and encouragement with your search and possible leads. Mailing lists and newsgroups exist for almost any professional group or interest category you can imagine. Chat rooms and forums are another way to network with professionals in your industry or occupation. The Riley Guide suggests using these services to find chats and forums in your area of interest:

- Vault.com
- Lycos Communities
- MSN Groups
- America Online (for AOL members only)

Joining free or low-cost job-search groups in your area is another way to connect with people going through a similar experience. These groups usually meet weekly for an hour to participate in moderated discussions, offer each other advice, or hear presentations from recruiters, employers, and other relevant speakers. Joining such a group is a good way to get out of the house and out of your own problems, especially if you use the meetings as a chance to help others as well as yourself. You can find a list of these clubs in CareerJournal.com's Calendar of Career Events (www.careerjournal.com/calendar/index.html).

FINDING JOB LISTINGS ON THE WEB

There are infinite ways to find job listings on the Internet. As Tim notes, you can register with leading job-posting sites, such as Monster.com; with industry-specific employment sites; or at sites designed for people at your level or in your function; you can also review job postings on company websites.

Although there are always exceptions, seeking out and responding to postings is probably the least effective use of your time, for the reasons Tim outlined and others. For instance, many postings are outdated or are somewhat low-level.

Don't count on getting too far with the online listings posted on the corporate websites of many large U.S. companies. Often, their listings are out of date or hard to locate. Many insist that job hunters complete long applications online. After spending time filling out the forms, some job hunters find the links break down and they can't submit their applications.

One need not be job hunting for long to discover the limitations of most corporate websites. As this job seeker observed:

The one frustrating thing I've discovered is that if an employer has a website, it generally wants you to submit your application online. Let's not even go into the employers whose online job-application forms don't work. They won't even talk to you or let you talk to someone without an appointment generated by them calling you first. —JG

But the knowledge that a company had an opening or is expanding a certain department can help you to focus your efforts. If you learn there's an opening that suits your skills, find out which person at the company you should contact directly about it. Then send a personalized letter and résumé to that person and follow up with a phone call. One job hunter explained his technique:

I was a post–September 11 casualty from a large computer-equipment manufacturer and although still unemployed, I've enjoyed (?) more than a dozen firm interview experiences solely from online postings—and email/telephone follow-up—that went directly through companies' own websites. Even if I see an appealing opening on a job board like Monster.com, I still use that info as a tip to go directly to the employer's website. There I have access to a wealth of info that helps me personalize my submission.

Many of the companies on my information-technology target list (about 300 firms classified as A, B, or C for closeness to my preferred company) also give names and email addresses (found in the job postings themselves or in press releases I've scoured) and also provide departments or organizational units and executives for the postings I respond to (located in company press releases as well). The websites also give the phone numbers for my follow-up a few days later. —Jim F.

AN ALTERNATIVE TO THE BIG JOB SITES

Some career counselors recommend that job hunters avoid large commercial job boards altogether in favor of a highly targeted approach that connects their desired work opportunity with companies that might provide it. When you know the two or three things you'd like to do and where you want to live, start researching using your favorite search engine. Type in words such as "business directory" and the location and you'll retrieve hundreds of listings about employers in that area. One job hunter had had success this way:

One method I used to find companies was going to Google.com and typing, for example, "project manager and Chicago." Or take a keyword from your résumé and do a search for that in Google. In my job search, I found a lot of companies using this method. —Camilla

After learning about such employers, start networking to find the names of people who might be in a position to hire you. Then write or call to introduce yourself as someone who can help that company to achieve its expansion, new product, financial, legal, or other goals.

If you simply want to find the names of companies in your industry that you don't know about, here are three websites offering a wealth of free information for job seekers:

- www.hoovers.com. Its Industry Masterlist catalogs companies by industry—in more than 300 industries. Plus, it has an A-to-Z company index and lists by region.
- www.thomasregister.com. A well-known print directory, Thomas Register lists more than a hundred thousand manufacturers by product, geographic location, and company data. Its website allows free access to company information if you register online.
- www.forbes.com. Forbes magazine produces several lists that can be a launching pad for active job seekers—for example, the Largest Private Companies, the 200 Best Small Companies, and the Forbes International 500, to name just a few.

ADVICE FROM THE TRENCHES

Of course, when it comes to Internet job hunting there are myriad other strategies. Participants in Tim's discussion board wrote in with suggestions on the best ways to use information gleaned from job postings and company sites to advance their search:

Most company recruiters who use the Internet to see résumés look only at those posted in the last week, so be sure to update your résumé often. If a website notifies you that your résumé has been read, be sure to send a hard copy to the company's human-resources department. Most large companies have their own online site, which includes available jobs. Be sure you send your résumé even if you aren't applying for a specific job. Sometimes timing is everything. —Rich R.

If your Internet-service provider offers personal Web space, create an online résumé that search engines can pick up. Most important, keep the CV up to date—and there are some job boards (CareerBuilder.com in particular) that require you to "edit" your résumé (change a word or two) every day or so to pick up hits. —Arne B.

Go to Monster.com or another big board and build search profiles. Within a couple of days, identify keywords for your online résumés. Use these online boards to identify jobs you want to do. Regional searches (for example, [Tim] would want to look in the Trenton, New Jersey, area) help identify interesting positions and provide an idea of the prerequisites. Tweak your résumé to emphasize matches between your skills and the employer's needs, then email it. Note the company and put it on a research list for review.

Finally, use companies' "résumé builders" and put yourself online. Using keywords and focused résumés, let the technology work for you. Select options allowing you to screen potential matches. When matches interest you, send your résumé. —Preston H.

If your job-search strategy isn't producing results, you'll need to try something new. Remember, the Internet is only one tool in your job-search toolbox. Other tools include direct contact (cold calling), job fairs, temping, and working with recruiters. The most successful job seekers use a mix of tactics. The drawbacks of relying on the Internet alone are readily apparent to anyone who's done it for any length of time, as this job hunter wrote:

I am totally burned out by trying to search online, but sometimes it seems like the only source for information. What's worse than ever, though, is that you don't even get the automated responses anymore. It seems like the minute you hit "send," the résumé goes to some vast wasteland. It's worse than rejection. How is a job hunter today to know if not getting a response is due to you or the system? —Nicole

RECRUITERS AND THE INTERNET

Perhaps the most elusive "animal" to stalk on the Internet is the executive recruiter. Most recruiting firms have created websites where they often list new recruiting assignments and encourage candidates to mail résumés. But don't expect to hear from a recruiter or firm you've emailed. Typically, search firms set up an assortment of email boxes, and the one that candidates are invited to respond to is an administrative receptacle. Periodically, lower-level staff will go through the résumés the search firm has received in this mailbox and either file or discard them. Rarely does a résumé actually make it to the desk of a recruiter doing a current search.

As Atlanta recruiter William M. Handler told a reporter in an interview with CareerJournal.com: "The likelihood that any recruiter or retained-search firm can assist someone in a job search is very remote. The probability is almost nonexistent that the person is going to be available for a job at the same time that we have a [suitable] opening. Generally, [unsolicited emails or letters] go to some kind of administrator, researcher, or clerical person who can make a preliminary decision about whether a résumé is worth retaining. Then it gets passed along to a mid-level researcher who will make a decision as to whether an individual is worth pursuing. The vast majority of résumés we get—and I'm sure that all the other firms get—don't get [assigned to a database]. Frankly, they get tossed. The volume is just too heavy to deal with, and other resources are available that help us pinpoint people who specifically have the experience we want."

Of course, there are always exceptions. Those with financial resources may want to purchase a database of recruiters in a specific function, industry, or geographic area and mass-mail their résumés. At least one job seeker on the discussion board says this tactic works:

> . . . My advice: Purchase a database of retained recruiters who specialize in your work. Use Microsoft Word to create a customized, signed letter for each recruiter with his or her name, correct title, etc. Send at least two thousand letters and your résumé—all at once. You will receive ten replies and get four interviews and one or two job offers. This might cost $1,500, but it beats unemployment. It worked for me, landing me a $170,000-a-year job in just eight weeks! —P. M.

Customized lists of recruiters can be purchased from Kennedy Information Inc. (www.kennedyinfo.com) and other sources.

TOO MUCH OF A GOOD THING?

The Internet is more akin to a living, breathing organism than to a library research section. At times, its greatest strength—providing detailed information on almost any topic available—is its greatest drawback. So make time management a priority when you're online. Also remember to take what you read online with a grain of salt—not all facts are checked or updated as quickly as they should be. Still, with a standard Internet connection, you can be highly informed about companies and ready to interview; get in touch and share information with other job seekers; and send out résumés—all without even leaving your house.

● ● ●

Most complaints about online job hunting have their counterparts in the "offline" world. If your search is going nowhere and you're not getting offers, it's a signal that you need to rethink your strategy. We can't overstress that personal networking is the most effective job-search method—and the best networking occurs in person.

CHAPTER 5

MONEY IS A TOUCHY SUBJECT
FOR JOBLESS PROFESSIONALS

- Computers Make It Seem Easy
- Keeping Cool About Finances
- Family Concerns
- Money-Management Tips

- Talking to Creditors
- Stretching a Dollar
- Know Your Worth

April 30

I've avoided writing about money thus far for several reasons. First, unemployment doesn't do good things for one's finances. Second, the rules of our culture dictate that it's crass to talk about money. Third, issues of money are closely intertwined with all sorts of psychological baggage.

For me, there's a certain unreality about money. For example, no matter how much I earn, I always seem to have about the same standard of living. I know there are many people far less fortunate than I for whom every penny matters. I also know an immutable law of prosperity: the less you own, the less you have to lose. So it's best to travel light. (When my first marriage ended and we sold our house, I had to dump two-thirds of my property to move into a small apartment. I didn't miss any of it.)

There are real, concrete issues as well. My wife and I have several thousand dollars of monthly expense before we buy so much as a loaf of bread.

WHERE WE STAND

For starters, we're locked into an apartment lease in Boston, which is one reason we're staying with my in-laws in Princeton, New Jersey. With the Boston rental market as soft as ripe Brie, we may have to pay out the entire lease, which expires in September. When we call real-estate agents to inquire about prospective tenants, they say, "You're still paying rent? Leases are broken all the time." Yes, they're broken frequently, apparently because a lot of people don't care about their credit rating or are willing to risk ruining it. We can't afford that.

Health insurance is nonnegotiable, especially since I have a family to protect.

Then there are school loans. Though I received a substantial scholarship for my M.B.A., the cost of living in Boston was so great that I'm carrying more debt than I've ever had. The federal government is kind enough to let me defer payment on my student loans, but the interest still accrues. (I wonder if they can repossess what's in my head?)

Day care for our daughter Hannah, we reasoned, is a necessity. Without it, my wife, who is a freelance editor, would never get any work done (we need her income), or I'd spend time taking care of Hannah rather than looking for a job. And Hannah wouldn't be able to play with other children regularly. My in-laws are chipping in to help with this expense, which makes me feel alternately loved and ashamed.

FEARING THE "WHAT IFS"

Not only do I have to think about the money we're spending, I also have to think about the money we aren't saving. If I listen to financial experts such as syndicated columnist Jane Bryant Quinn, I should be saving $200 a day for my year-old daughter's college fund. (OK, maybe it's more like $200 a month.) Even when we're flush, we aren't socking away this kind of money.

If you believe these financial gurus, every American is supposed to put away a couple hundred a month from the time we're ten years old. If we don't, we'll have to live on the street because Social Security and Medicare will be bankrupt. I love reading the columns in which a twenty-three-year-old asks question about money or investing, and the expert's response begins with something like, "Don't worry. It's not too late to start saving for retirement." What planet are these people from?

Which brings me to the psychological baggage. Taking money from family makes my wife and me feel like children again. We'd rather not do it, but we don't think we have a choice. I'm also taking money from the unemployment office, which is easier than taking money from family, except that every person who comes into contact with the checks or the postcards that I must submit every other week learns that I'm unemployed. Since we're establishing residence in a new state, there are countless forms to complete. As if to taunt me, each form asks for my employer and work phone number. Even the checkout person at the supermarket where I applied for a discount card knows I'm jobless.

I went to see a doctor for a routine checkup. I left the employer portion of the form blank. The receptionist shouted across the waiting room: "Who's your employer?" I shouted back: "I'm unemployed." People buried their heads in their magazines.

When I have to actually say the words, I get a variety of responses. Some people plow ahead as though they haven't heard what I said. Others turn a sad face. The people who have been there offer cheerful support. I've raised not caring to a high art; how else could I write this column? I see articles on a regular basis claiming there's no shame in being unemployed these days because of the millions of layoffs taking place. And yet there's a nagging voice that tells me I am what I produce—no more or less. Is this a male thing?

Finally, there's the issue of need versus worth. Should need determine salary or should worth? Need is sort of nebulous; if the best things in life are free, how much does anyone truly need? Does anyone really need a BMW? It's much easier to estimate worth. Job-hunting books encourage us to "monetize" our value to the company when negotiating salary. That sort of pure free-market thinking allows CEOs, movie stars, and athletes to command millions, because they generate more than that in revenue. Teachers, therefore, really don't deserve a living wage.

The chairman of AT&T Corp. was paid $4 million in salary and bonus in 2001 while the company's stock declined in value by almost 40 percent, prompting the board to call for the first reverse split of a Dow component. Yes, the telecom industry has had a tough time in general, but shouldn't the chairman be held accountable for at least part of the problem? I'm sure I could do an equally poor job for millions less.

KEEPING COOL ABOUT FINANCES

Finances are among the top worries after a job loss. Fears that normally remain in check can run amok. How will you be able to pay your bills? How will you make ends meet? Even level-headed people may find it difficult to think clearly about their financial situation after they've lost a job. It's no surprise Tim had avoided the unpleasant task of writing about money problems until well into his search.

Why do money matters heighten your emotional vulnerability? A job loss can upset your daily structure, sense of control, and self-esteem. Earning and spending is a strong source of gratification and power for most people. Job hunters on the discussion board offered their own advice for coping:

Try not to focus too much on the psychological baggage of taking money from others. I'm sure you've been there for people in need when you could—I can say this for myself—so don't condemn yourself for now being in this position. Yes, we must be productive. However, how much "productivity" would you demand from, say, someone with multiple sclerosis? Is such a person less worthy of respect because of an "inability to produce"?

I won't even touch the issue of worth as related to career or position. It's based on too many subjectives. One thing I suggest: are you a member of a church or any support group? My church has been one of the few places where my worth hasn't depended on what I make—or don't. —Justin

Nearly all layoff victims probably can relate to Tim's complex feelings about money, but seldom do they talk about them.

I thought I was the only one who thought (and lived) this way. That part about having to pay other obligations before buying a loaf of bread was exactly right. —Herb W.

It may be helpful to air your feelings with a friend or counselor. Financial issues are a source of conflicts in many families, and these problems are likely to intensify. You may find that a seemingly innocent comment can cause a major argument.

FAMILY CONCERNS

Don't hide the news about your job loss from your loved ones. Following layoffs or firings, a surprising number of people pretend to still be working and leave for the "office" at the same time every day. Have an honest discussion with your spouse or partner, and include your children in this conversation. Many people think it's better if kids don't know about financial problems. However, children can sense things aren't the same and may think the situation is worse than it is. Discuss how you plan to handle the situation and how family members can help if necessary.

Because money is often tied to power in relationships, the loss of a paycheck can precipitate a change in established patterns and cause problems for couples. In some relationships, the person who earns the most is the power broker. After a job loss, one or both partners may feel a new or greater need to be the financial watchdog. Resentment can build when record-keeping is challenged or explanations are required where none were before. But if neither partner wants the watchdog role, bills may accumulate, and arguments over who's to blame may follow. When emotions are running high, it can be tough to establish new rules for spending. And the new rules can cause problems until each person becomes comfortable with the new arrangement.

Above all, it's important to communicate regularly and openly. Make a plan for your finances as soon as possible, and try to separate emotional issues from financial realities. While this may be difficult, deferring talk about money may lead only to more difficulties. When these issues are resolved, you may find your relationships become healthier as a result, as this job seeker reports:

My wife and I have shared a valuable transition in our marriage partnership. We are closer because of this phase of my career. My wife has become the income generator for us. This has been very beneficial for her. It has given her even more self-esteem, and she has risen to the task. While my father-in-law struggles with the macho viewpoint that I have failed because the woman has become the provider, I am pleased that she has the opportunity to feel the pride she feels. —Doug T.

MONEY-MANAGEMENT TIPS

Ideally, you'll have savings set aside for a rainy day, but even a sizable nest egg may not be enough to see you through to your next job. And nowadays many folks carry a sizable debt burden, which can add to the strain. So analyze your financial situation. Add up your basic cost-of-living outlays and fixed expenses: mortgage, rent, utilities, and the like. Next, add up your available liquid assets and sources of income. Don't forget to include any severance or unemployment payments you'll be receiving, interest and dividends on investments, and your spouse's income. Then create a revised spending plan that takes into account how long you realistically expect your job search to last.

Unless you aren't receiving severance or your expenses exceed your income, you may not need to cut back right away. But don't make any major purchases or take expensive vacations. Simply adopt a more modest lifestyle— without overdoing it.

Decide which bills to pay first. For example, never pay an unsecured debt, such as a credit-card bill, before paying a secured debt, such as your mortgage or auto loan. You'll still need a place to live and a means of transportation. Reduce any automatic payments you make to savings accounts or investments, such as mutual funds.

When drawing up a budget, it's a good idea to have another discussion with the whole family. Have every member of the family make a list of spending priorities and possible cutbacks. Each person should express his or her feelings about losses, needs, and wishes. Listen without arguing. Then identify common ground, agree on reductions, and finalize your monthly budget.

TALKING TO CREDITORS

It's also a good idea to talk with creditors about more favorable repayment terms. Explain that you've lost your job and ask for a reduction in interest rates or payments until you're reemployed. It's wise to take this step before you fall behind. Keep written records of all your conversations and any new agreements.

If you're facing delinquency on your home, contact the lender—the earlier, the better. Many are amenable to working with mortgage holders, especially if circumstances are temporary. Remember, the lender is better off if you stay in your home. Some lenders offer "workout" plans that vary from extending the length of the payment period to allowing a homeowner to suspend payment until reemployment. A variety of public-private partnerships and state agencies have programs for homeowners facing or already in delinquency.

(If you're still employed, consider applying for a home-equity loan. You may need to tap into the funds eventually, and it's difficult to get a line of credit without a job.)

Consider your health-insurance options. See if your spouse's plan will cover you, or apply through your company for coverage under COBRA (the Consolidated Omnibus Budget Reconciliation Act). This allows you to pay group rates to keep all or some of your former employer's health benefits for at least eighteen months. However, many newly unemployed people are stunned to learn the cost of COBRA coverage. It might make more sense to buy an individual plan with a higher deductible but with much lower premiums.

Don't raid your 401(k) or other qualified retirement plan. If you're under age fifty-nine and a half, you'll pay income taxes and a 10 percent penalty on the withdrawals. If needed, you may get an exception for a "hardship withdrawal" necessary to pay for medical expenses for you, your spouse, or your dependents, or for other emergencies.

STRETCHING A DOLLAR

Don't cut back on expenses that could improve your job prospects. For example, don't forgo the daily babysitter if it means you'll have to stay home instead of looking for work. An easy way to save money is to eat out less often or to choose less expensive restaurants. Impulse snack purchases also mount up; consider skipping those lattés or other pricey treats. Try to buy staple items in bulk when they're on sale. Save money on utilities by turning out lights when you leave a room; turning the thermostat down in the winter or up in the summer; or switching to a phone carrier willing to give you a better deal.

Your job loss may make you eligible for discounts from your local gym, professional organization, cellular phone service, software retailer, or vendors offering private instruction, such as guitar lessons or yoga classes. These may be unadvertised specials or cloaked in euphemistic terms, such as "alumni rates." They may be doled out on a case-by-case basis only, so to learn about them, you may have to ask.

If you have trouble sticking to your budget, get a notebook and write down everything you spend in a given week. This will help you spot problem areas and reduce spending. Consider accepting a part-time job or taking on consulting projects while you're unemployed. These stints could also give your résumé a needed boost.

When money gets tight, moving in with parents to save money, as Tim and his wife did, isn't uncommon. But this solution can, of course, trigger its own host of problems.

I lost my job with a Big Five firm back in April 2001 and, oh, how my world crumbled! I am currently doing independent consulting, but have since moved back into my mother's house. It isn't an easy experience, and I've asked myself many times how I ever survived living with my mother all my growing years. I don't wish this predicament on my future kids. —Kelly M. T.

Relocating to a less expensive part of the country was the answer for one job seeker, even though he didn't have a new job waiting for him in his new location:

My wife and I decided that, since we don't work on Wall Street, but live in a very high-cost New Jersey suburb and have an enormous amount of equity in our house, we would move to a less expensive area with no mortgage. Living in an area like New York, Boston, or Silicon Valley, we forget that most of the rest of the country still has shortages of skilled professionals with the competitive backgrounds we have had to work in major markets. I know people who have gone to places like Rochester, New York; Omaha, Nebraska; St. Louis, Minneapolis, and Houston who make 70 to 80 percent of the money, but have a much better lifestyle. I stayed in the New York City area for all these years believing that this was the one place I could always find the right job. I recently bought a house in North Carolina and am now looking for employment there. —Robert J.

KNOW YOUR WORTH

Don't let your unemployed status put you at a disadvantage when you do get that job offer. While you may feel that you lack leverage to bargain with employers, it may help to know that there's an art to negotiating pay. Make sure you get a fair compensation package. (For more on negotiating, see chapter 12.) If your search is prolonged, you may be tempted to grab the first offer you receive, just to restore your family's financial security. But remember, if you take a job you aren't happy with, you may find yourself back in the job market before long.

To be sure, finances are fraught with emotional issues. Still, money doesn't have to be the bugaboo it becomes for many people. Once you've faced the reality of the issues head-on, you can emerge stronger on the other side.

● ● ●

Tim's job loss forced him to examine his feelings about money, and he and his wife were able to work out a plan for spending. Even so, the experience wasn't without its accompanying baggage. But by planning ahead and recognizing the sensitivities involved, you may find that your finances and your personal relationships can survive through your job search.

CHAPTER 6

A CANDIDATE'S NOVEL STRATEGY FOR INTERVIEWING: BE YOURSELF

- How Job Seekers View Interviewing

- Expect "Zero Feedback"

- Have the Right Mindset

- Be Likeable

- Be a "Can-Do" Person

- Do Your Homework

- Do You Look the Part?

- Ready Your Answers

- Recruiters' Favorites

- Curve Balls

- Behavioral Questions

- Illegal Questions

- Ask Your Own Questions

- The Salary Issue

- Like the Dating Game

May 18

I've been reading books and articles about interviewing, and they can make me nuts. The authors seem to suggest that if I wear the right thing, say the right thing, and act and react the right way, I can force people to give me the job I covet. I should be able to win every time, which makes me think that every time I begin an interview, my entire fate is in my hands.

Do people really memorize stock answers from these books and try to deliver them so that they sound fresh and natural? Do the suggested strategy games and cute attention-getting tricks really work? In an anecdote from one book I read, the kid in the mailroom of an ad agency sent the CEO a dead fish with a clever headline attached. Of course, he got the job he wanted. Today, this type of stunt seems a little spooky. If you've read anything about interviews at consulting firms, you know how strange the questions can get: should I be prepared to tell an interviewer why manhole covers are round and how many ping-pong balls will fit into a Boeing 747?

Certainly, I want to put my best foot forward in an interview, but what does that mean? I don't get nervous very often in interviews, and, as a former actor, I feel confident that I can carry off any number of personas implicit in the suggestions of various interview experts. But my core question is this: should an interview be a great performance, a completely candid and spontaneous exchange, or something in between?

Let's face it: often, the success or failure of a particular interview is completely out of our hands. At a recent weekly meeting of JobSeekers—a local support group I've attended for the unemployed or those soon-to-be—a recruiter told the audience of sixty that he eliminated anyone who came to an interview dressed in a brown suit or wearing an unusual necktie. Why? Even he could not articulate the reason.

Other interviewers' standards may be just as arbitrary. Right out of business school, I had an interview at a well-known software company; I could tell I was finished before that interview even started. With my résumé in hand, the interviewer's opening observation was, "You've done a lot of nonprofit work. Why would anyone want to do that?" I responded with something about passion for mission, vision, and service. Then it got worse.

He told me about two positions for which he was considering me. "In job one, you'll never have enough resources, and you have to constantly browbeat overworked, depressed people into producing more. In job two, you'll deal directly with clients who are usually angry and disappointed, and who will always want more than you can provide. Does either of these sound appealing to you?" This is what I call a nice setup. If I said, "They both sound great!" I'd seem like a liar or an idiot. And if I got a job by being someone other than myself, would I eventually hate it? My response was, "Well, you make it very difficult to resist, but thanks very much for your time." I didn't know what was going on there, but I thought it best to cut my losses and move on.

LUCK AND CHEMISTRY

The best and worst thing about interviewers is that they're human beings. Each has his or her own biases, which means that luck and chemistry are important factors in a successful interview. The interviewer must like you. Still, I figure that there are some universal "don'ts." I assume that making jokes about death or Star Trek is unwise. So, too, are behavioral extremes, such as begging or crying. But within these boundaries, there's a lot of latitude. So how do you decide what's appropriate?

For my own sanity, I try to keep it simple. In an interview, I:

- Do my research beforehand
- Am relaxed but alert
- Maintain eye contact
- Smile warmly
- Listen carefully and enthusiastically
- Try to ask intelligent questions
- Make occasional notes
- Follow up afterward with a thank-you letter

Other than that, I'm pretty spontaneous.

So what about results? After a long dry spell I recently had interviews at three organizations: an advertising agency, a publishing company, and a consulting firm. I thought they all went very well, thank you.

In my meetings at the advertising agency, I was so relaxed that I think the hiring manager was concerned: he asked me about my energy level. He may be used to talking with business-development people who are always wound up. From my acting experience, I can be completely comfortable and relaxed in all situations. I'm alert and attentive and have fire in my eyes, but I'm not strung out. Maybe certain interviewers need to see some evidence of jitters to believe you really want the job. I knew I wasn't getting a callback when I saw the position posted on HotJobs.com after my first interview. The posting said they were looking for someone with more direct agency experience. Perhaps. But perhaps being completely relaxed isn't always a plus.

BONDING BY CURSING

My first interview at the publishing company was with its president. He actually told me that he liked me because I always looked him in the eye. I think he also liked that I swore. He'd brandished the f-word when he called me to set up the interview, so I let loose with a couple of words of my own. This could easily have backfired, but I was able to carry it off, because I normally swear like a sailor anyway. For two and a half hours we had a great time envisioning the future of the company. After a second interview with him and another with the vice president, the president told me that he really liked me. He said that while I had more vision than any of the other candidates, I lacked the right background for this particular job, but he wanted to keep in touch. He was concerned that I might have a learning curve. In this tight market, he wanted a perfect fit. We had great chemistry, and I still didn't get the f-ing job.

At the consulting firm, I interviewed with its HR consultant, who was looking for a marketing director. He actually spent the first ten minutes making fun of the schools I'd attended. (I'd learned from the firm's website that its main selling point was the Ivy League pedigree of its consultants.) He said I'd done well on the hour-long reasoning test I'd just taken: "If you hadn't, we wouldn't even be talking. If you're stupid, we can't use you." I passed the screening interview but didn't make the cut to see the president; I don't have Ivy League credentials, which apparently isn't OK with him. Strategy and posturing didn't matter here; I was done before I started.

Actors often turn themselves inside out trying to be what they think the casting people want. After all, they're actors. But the irony is that successful actors are usually successful because they bring their true selves into the roles they play. I'd be thrilled if interviewers could tell me the truth about why I didn't get the job, and if I could believe that what they tell me is the truth. But I've been on the hiring side; I never told applicants that they weren't hired because I thought they seemed crazy, strange, stupid, or lazy—and various interviewees were some or all of these things. So I know that I'm

HOW JOB SEEKERS VIEW INTERVIEWING

Like Tim, many job hunters regard interviewing as a necessary evil that can't be avoided in their quest for a job. No matter how hard they tried to win over interviewers, they feel the deck is always stacked against them. The comments this topic drew on Tim's discussion board reflect this sentiment:

I have never seen anything like this in my life. I thought this willingness to waste a job seeker's time sending him on a runaround was just in South Florida. When I find myself jumping through too many hoops (three references—no, five references; no writing sample; no grant sample; no, that ad was a mistake), I stop. —Michael C.

My experience has taught me that unless you match the position perfectly, you won't even get a call. If you do, you will have to compete with twenty or more candidates. So it will all boil down to whether the hiring manager likes you. At best it's a crapshoot—even if you are qualified and are the best candidate. It seems like many human-resources people are trying to justify their existence, so they interview far too many people for even the simplest of positions. —Randy M.

Still, if you're persistent, patient, strategic, and thoughtful about your search campaign, you'll eventually hear from an interviewer. Being invited to meet with company representatives will naturally raise your hopes. But when jobs are scarce, employers can afford to be choosy. When they don't fear candidates will accept other offers, they'll wait to find one who meets their entire "wish list" of requirements for the opening. In contrast, when candidates are scarce, companies might settle for those who meet 75 percent or less of the wish list.

One candidate wrote to the discussion group to say the process is like competing on a TV reality show:

There are hundreds of résumés being submitted for any particular job. I spoke with a human-resources executive who indicated that his company received more than six hundred résumés for one position. He culled it down to a hundred or so based on a keyword search, then read those. He ended up inviting about twenty or so people in for interviews and narrowed it down to six or seven for the hiring executive to meet. I feel like the odds are close to those for winning the big Power Ball lottery.

Another company invited me in for an interview for a vice president of marketing position. The employer neglected to mention that it had invited about twenty-five other people in at the same time for a "group interview." I stayed for the experience, and because I was curious. We each had a chance to speak twice, then the interviewer had the nerve to ask us to state why we were the best candidate for the job—but if we weren't selected who else in the room we thought was a good candidate. I guess the management there must have been a fan of *Survivor.* —Susan O.

EXPECT "ZERO FEEDBACK"

What seems to bother job hunters most is their lack of control over the process. They hate not hearing back from interviewers—even when they aren't chosen. Many Diary participants landed their last jobs at a time when companies had larger human resources staffs and contacted unsuccessful applicants.

I have been looking for a job for the past year and am completely shocked to see how human-resources departments have been working. I am in the HR field and have been interviewing with companies that don't bother to follow up with a candidate after an interview—even if the candidate flies across the country to interview. I have been referred by internal employees of companies, and I don't even get so much as a courtesy phone call providing any kind of status. Not even, "We have your résumé—don't call us, we'll call you!" —Marty E.

I, too, was struck by how it was possible to get zero feedback even after traveling a long distance for an interview. I kind of accepted that it was in my best interest to assume the burden of follow-up as much as possible, but I still was in disbelief about how little effort employers felt they could (evidently, in good conscience) get away with. I guess I choose to believe that people were simply crazy-busy and overwhelmed. Thinking that way makes me feel better than believing that they were intentionally callous. —uptown123

HAVE THE RIGHT MINDSET

Perhaps the best way to keep your sanity and lower your frustration during the interviewing phase is to tell yourself:

- Interviewing is a continuation of the job-search "numbers game"; the more interviewers you meet with, the sooner you will find a new position.
- Interviewing, like job hunting generally, isn't personal. No interviewer can make a decision about you as a person in the short time you are together. There's no need to feel you are "lesser than" or deficient in any way because you aren't chosen.
- It's unlikely you'll hear from the interviewer. As layoffs continue to decimate staffs and everyone is expected to do more with less, hiring managers and human-resources personnel don't have time to follow up with applicants. They aren't rewarded for such acts of kindness, only for bringing in more candidates for interviews, so there is no incentive (other than courtesy) for them to do so.

As one job seeker told the Diary discussion group:

Many years ago, I was blessed to work for a manager who supplied me with a secret question when I wanted to understand why something happens in the workplace. And here it is: "What is being rewarded?" So let's think about the treatment of job candidates. Is proficient, timely, and polite feedback with prospective employees rewarded in the workplace? Sadly, no. The task of hiring people is an extremely thankless and unrewarding one. You can go through eighty applicants, yet have absolutely nothing to show for it until the actual position is filled. Meanwhile, you have mountains of tasks that need immediate attention. —Questing Elf

BE LIKEABLE

Even if interviewing can be a thankless endeavor, you still need to go all out to be successful at it. As much as possible, you must present yourself as someone whom the interviewer can imagine working with. Despite all kinds of attempts to make interviewing a more objective process, it isn't! Studies show that interviewers are most comfortable hiring candidates who are more like than unlike them and whom they would enjoy as colleagues. This sometimes may be described as "fit": "Would he fit in here?" "Would she be a good addition to our group?" "Could I stand to work with him every day?" "How would she get along with Annie and Bob?" "Does he or she have the kind of values that match our own?"

Ways to improve your likeability quotient include the following:

- Maintaining good eye contact with the interviewer
- Smiling and otherwise demonstrating good humor
- Listening and communicating well
- Being interested in the interviewer without being intrusive
- Showing confidence and a positive attitude
- Not talking negatively about past employers, bosses, or coworkers
- Demonstrating excitement about the opportunity
- Not showing too much self-interest
- Being pleasant to everyone you meet

BE A "CAN-DO" PERSON

It's been said that companies don't hire people, they hire *solutions*. You must appear to be the solution to the problem the job is designed to solve. On your résumé, you've shown you have the skills and background to meet the job's requirements. Now it's a matter of verifying in person that you're the man or woman to resolve the company's current headache.

In this regard, most interviewers, corporate recruiters, and hiring managers start with certain minimum expectations of candidates:

- They want candidates to be informed about their organizations
- They expect interviewees to dress appropriately
- They want to be asked questions and hear comments that show a personal desire to be hired by this company, for this job

DO YOUR HOMEWORK

An informed candidate will always come across better in interviews than someone who knows nothing about the company. While you don't need to be an expert on the firm, you should know certain basics, such as:

- Ownership of the company, division, or group, if it isn't a stand-alone entity

- The products the company makes or the services it provides
- The names of the president, the chairman, and the executive overseeing the department you'd work in
- The company's recent financial performance record—whether it has been profitable and whether the stock is trading above or below recent levels
- Names of competitors and an understanding of the company's strengths in relation to them
- Recent and upcoming developments
- Where the opening you want fits into the organization chart
- The required skills and the demands of the opening
- Some understanding of the company's history and general philosophy

Review the ad or online posting to learn as much as you can about the job. Ask for any additional material about it to be sent to you ahead of time. As mentioned in chapter 4, you can learn pertinent facts about companies by exploring their websites or by reviewing online business directories, such as www.hoovers.com. Most company websites archive recent news releases, officer biographies, and product or service descriptions. Take note of things you come across that you might like to discuss with the interviewer. Being observant and offering insightful comments can make you memorable.

If the company is listed on a general business-directory site, you'll find facts about its sales, number of employees, locations, top officers, products, list of competitors, names of subsidiaries, and where it stands in the industry.

Learn about the company's stock performance on a brokerage or general news site that publishes stock-market information. Most business-news websites provide such data.

Perhaps the most important sources of information are your personal contacts. Call your relevant professional or industry association and ask to speak with someone who might be able to tell you about the company. Ask around for referrals to people who might work there. Call and explain that you have been invited to interview for a job at the company and that you'd greatly appreciate it if they could spare a few minutes to discuss the employer with you. Then ask general questions that might help with your interview.

After all this effort, the interviewer may not want to know about anything you've learned. But there's always a chance he or she will lean back and say, "Tell me, what do you know about our organization?" In this case, a blank stare and a lame, "Well, I like your products," will earn you a quick dismissal, say recruiters. For instance, Amy Barnhart, manager of recruitment for television broadcaster ABC Inc. in New York, says she's continually "amazed" when candidates she meets with "don't even know that ABC is owned by Disney."

DO YOU LOOK THE PART?

It goes without saying that you should look your best in interviews. Let interviewers see that you can make appropriate decisions about your attire and would be a good representative for the organization. The rule of thumb is to always dress one level up from what your future coworkers might be wearing. As Marky Stein remarks in *Fearless Interviewing* (Writers Club Press, 2001), "It is almost impossible to overdress for an interview unless you are wearing a tuxedo or beaded evening gown."

Don Asher, author of *The Overnight Job Change Strategy* (Ten Speed Press, 1993), suggests visiting the employer's offices prior to your meeting to observe how employees are dressed. One candidate he knows borrowed a tweed jacket with suede elbow patches for a morning interview for a writing position and then changed into a black suit to apply for a financial job in the afternoon. "Appearance is critical," says Mr. Asher. "I have seen more than one candidate hired because she had the right look or the right suit."

Interviewers can be both catty and snobby. Your wardrobe and how much it cost may be dissected after you leave. Don't skimp on quality. Even if you can afford only one outfit, make it a good one. Fabrics should be natural, not synthetic. Collars can't be frayed. Shoes must be polished. Don't wear clothes that are too loose or tight: the fit must be perfect. Make sure your hair has been trimmed or shaped recently.

Older candidates, who may have years' worth of business clothes in their closets, should particularly heed this advice. Interviewers will scrutinize your appearance for signs that you aren't "in touch" or current on clothing trends. Buy yourself a new interview outfit. If you need advice on what to choose, talk to friends and colleagues and take them shopping with you if necessary.

If you are dressed well, you will feel better about yourself and exude more confidence during the interview. As Sue T. wrote to Tim:

I think the most important thing in finding a new job is energy and a positive attitude. When I'm perky and have on a cute outfit, my interviews are the best.

READY YOUR ANSWERS

The good news, says Philadelphia career counselor Douglas B. Richardson, is that there are only two interview questions; that is, regardless of what you're asked, the employer really only wants to know:

1. What value can you add to my enterprise as an employee (and can you prove it)?
2. Why do you want this job?

Every interview question probes some dimension of your capability or motivation. The problem is that interviewers sometimes ask questions without knowing why they're asking them. Moreover, some questions shouldn't be taken at face value. Your challenge is to build a coherent picture of your strengths and figure out the interviewer's real intent.

Practice in advance for the likely questions that will come your way during the meeting. Interviewers have been known to ramble on the entire time and may not ask you anything. But chances are that they'll ask one or more of these common inquiries:

- Tell me about yourself.
- What in your background has prepared you for this opening?
- Why should we hire you?
- Where do you see yourself in three to five years?
- Why do you want to work here?
- What are your greatest weaknesses?
- What are your greatest strengths?
- Why are you job hunting?
- Why did you leave your last position?
- What would your subordinates say about you?
- What would your last boss say about you?
- Do you have any questions?

RECRUITERS' FAVORITES

Executive recruiters are known to go beyond these basics. The following is a sampling of some of their favorite questions for top-level candidates that they've shared with CareerJournal.com. As you peruse the list, consider what insights recruiters are probing for when they ask such questions and prepare your responses accordingly.

- What is the biggest misperception people have about you?
- What motivates you in your work life?
- If your internal business clients were going to spend money on your training and development, what might they spend it on?
- What do you do to have fun?
- What did your father do for a living?
- What specific accomplishments and experience do you have that would give my clients supreme confidence that their most critical objective can be reached?
- Tell me about the key experiences and relationships of the past that have been instrumental in your becoming who you are today.
- How many times in your career have you settled for second best?
- Tell me about a business relationship that blew up. Which part was your fault?
- Take me from college to the present in your career.
- Give me an example of when you should have communicated more information to the CEO, and you didn't. What happened and why?

CURVE BALLS

You may be asked questions that seem unfair, harsh, meaningless, or arbitrary. You may be tempted to fire back a rude answer, but hold your tongue. As Bob L. told the discussion group:

A casualty of the telecom meltdown, I have been out of work for nearly a year; 437 job applications later, I have had one on-site and two phone interviews. The last hiring manager asked me, 'What have you been doing all this time?' Needless to say, I didn't respond with the answer that was going through my mind.

Again, the best way to answer such questions is to first ask yourself, "What does the interviewer really want to know by asking me this?" Often, if you can determine the intent behind the query, you can allay the interviewers' concerns.

Say you're asked "Don't you believe you may be overqualified for this job?" According to career counselor Marky Stein, in asking this question, the interviewer really fears that (1) you may leave because you don't find the position challenging enough or (2) you may be unhappy with the salary the company is offering, ask for more money, or leave when you get a better offer. She suggests the following answer:

"After discussing the position with you and seeing the job description, I feel I have a good understanding about both the responsibilities of the job and the compensation. I feel comfortable with both and I'm eager to work for your company."

BEHAVIORAL QUESTIONS

Some of the most difficult questions candidates face today are those that start with such phrases as "Tell me about a time when . . ." or "Give me an example of . . .". This technique is known as behavioral interviewing; it is predicated on the belief that past performance is the best predictor of future success. Interviewers who favor this format usually develop their line of questioning around the traits and skills deemed important for success in the position or organization. For example, if a job involves a lot of customer service, an interviewer might ask you, "Tell me about a time when you had to handle an irate customer." For a position that requires extensive teamwork, you might be asked:

- "Give an example of a situation where you demonstrated your skill as a team player."
- "Tell me about a time when you had to rely on a team to get things done."
- "Provide an example of a time when you had to persuade people to do something that they didn't want to do."
- "Give me an example of your leadership style."

A behavioral interview might also include the following:

- Describe a problem or crisis you created and how you handled it.
- Describe a situation in which you made the wrong decision. What did you learn?
- Provide an example of a situation in which you failed or had less-than-desired results.
- Describe a problem you had with a former supervisor and how you dealt with it.
- Tell me about a major failure in your life and how you dealt with it.

Typically, you'll do well by preparing three or more career success stories and two or more that had less-than-favorable outcomes but were learning experiences. Success stories are "Kodak moments" from your career—and the more recent, the better. Your résumé is a good source: look for promotions, raises, awards, evaluations, and successful projects. Also consider new business successes and other times you received special recognition.

For learning experiences, choose humbling events from earlier in your career that molded you into the experienced professional you are today.

Review your résumé and decide which stories to tell. Then write, edit, and rehearse your stories. That way you minimize the risk of drawing a blank, telling the wrong story, or rambling.

Compose your stories as if you were creating a thirty-second radio spot. Some counselors recommend using a Problem–Action–Result (PAR) formula to structure these stories. Use numbers whenever possible; for example, include details on increased revenue, profit, market share, and savings. Memorize your stories and perfect their delivery in front of a mirror or video camera. Your enthusiasm and emotional involvement with your employer should come through loud and clear.

When you're asked to tell one of your stories, connect the interviewer's questions with your message. These links aren't always needed, but when done well, they provide a seamless transition between the question and its answer. Successful politicians have perfected this technique of linking the questions they're asked with the messages they want to deliver. They can be observed plying their skills at news conferences and on Sunday morning TV talk shows.

Consider these useful links:

- "That's difficult to say, but let me tell you about a similar experience at . . .
- "That reminds me of the time when . . .
- "That resonates with the time that . . .
- "They would probably tell you about . . .
- "For example . . ."

Don't be afraid to ask for clarification, such as, "I'm not sure what kind of information you'd like me to provide here. Can you be more specific?" And, you can finish up the story or response by asking for feedback or clarification: "Is that the kind of example you were looking for?"

In using this technique, interviewers are probing to see if you have the right skills and traits for the job and how well you function under pressure. Candidates who understand behavioral interviewing and are prepared to handle these questions have an edge over those who are unaware of this trend and must be coached by interviewers to respond appropriately.

ILLEGAL QUESTIONS

Questions about your marital status, personal life, arrest record, physical or mental disabilities, race, religion, sexual preferences, or ethnicity are illegal, and most good recruiters won't ask them. However, they still may want to know things that relate to your ability to do the job.

> Illegal:
> *Are you married? Do you have children? Are you planning to have children?*
> *Do you have to care for any dependents?*
> Legal:
> *Will you be able to travel frequently to client locations?*
> Illegal:
> *Do you have a disability of any kind?*
> Legal:
> *Do you have any physical or mental condition that would prevent you*
> *from doing this job?*
> Illegal:
> *How do you feel about working with a gay person?*
> Legal:
> *Do you have difficulty working with any types of people?*

If an interviewer errs and asks you an illegal question, you have two choices: get up and leave or respond in a tactful way. Unless other red flags have been raised that make the job unattractive, choose the second option. For instance, you could say:

- "I'm not sure I understand what you mean. Can you rephrase the question?"
- "I am completely qualified for all aspects of this job. Is that what you want to know?"
- "Could you explain how this topic relates to the qualifications for the job?"

ASK YOUR OWN QUESTIONS

Near the end of the meeting, most interviewers will ask if there is anything you would like to know. Be prepared and ask several questions to demonstrate your interest. You might consider one of the following:

- How is performance rewarded here?
- Why is the position open?
- What is the organization's communication style?
- What types of values are prevalent in this company?
- What do you like most about working here?
- What areas of the company are expected to grow most in the future?
- What is the company's policy about promotions?
- What personal attributes are most critical for success in this job?
- Would you say that I meet the requirements of your ideal candidate?
- What is your timetable for making a decision on this?
- How would you like me to follow up with you about next steps?

THE SALARY ISSUE

From the comments Tim received in response to this installment, interview questions about salary requirements appear to be the biggest stumpers. Candidates say their meetings often are terminated abruptly if they don't answer these questions in initial interviews. Yet most are advised not to address this issue until an offer is on the table.

My personal favorite is the interview I went on where "good negotiating skills and experience" were a primary factor. In the first two minutes of the interview I was asked what my salary expectations were. My reply, based on the rather skimpy job description, was, "Can I defer answering until we discuss the position in depth?" The reply: "We don't want to proceed if you are expecting more than we are willing to offer." I pointed out that one of the primary responsibilities of the position was negotiating price with clients and said that I would never quote or negotiate without understanding the prime aspects of the client's requirements. The reply: "OK, I understand the situation. We'll let you know." That was in January; I'm not holding my breath. —Don B.

While I understand that it is premature to talk about money on the first call, it has become clear that callers are screening candidates on the basis of current salary. If you ask what the salary range is you will be politely informed that they "do not know." A few months back I received a screening call for a program-manager position. Everything went well until the last question: "How much do you make?" I said "market" and politely declined—several times—to provide a figure. Eventually, after a very long pause, I was informed that my résumé wouldn't be forwarded to the next level until I provided my current salary. Feeling like I was in a "Catch 22" situation, I provided the information requested—and informed the screening caller that it was negotiable. Needless to say, I never did hear back. —Julius A.

Job hunters who participated in the Diary discussion eventually came to this conclusion:

If a company insists on knowing a candidate's salary history before or during the first interview, it probably isn't a good place to work. (For more about how to handle pay negotiations, see chapter 12.)

I got through the first interview successfully deflecting the salary question. I was brought back as one of two to make it to the next round and was immediately confronted by the CEO and a principal investor, who demanded that I answer the question before we went any further. Needless to say, I didn't want to work for that company any more than they wanted me on their team after I told them that it was still too soon to discuss money. —Thatch

Last week I got a call from a human-resources person at a major defense contractor screening me for a job. Not even fifteen seconds into the conversation, I was hit with the salary history/requirement question. I'd tried to deter it by asking how much the position—which she didn't adequately describe—would pay. Her response was, "That is proprietary." To get the conversation moving again, I told her my most recent salary. On hearing it, she cut our conversation short. After thinking about this misadventure, it was probably best that our conversation ended quickly. Companies that are hypersensitive about salary probably aren't the best places to land if you are expecting to get your career back on track. —John I.

LIKE THE DATING GAME

Interviewing for jobs is akin to seeking a marriage partner. You have to go on lots of dates until you find the situation in which both sides know the chemistry is right. You can do many things to improve your chances, but at the end of the day, the equation for job-search success is often:

$$Luck + Preparation = Opportunity$$

• • •

Resourceful people can create their own luck by asking questions, seeking out ways to meet others, volunteering to help whenever possible, and looking for something new in every occasion. Try to create your own luck in your job search and be as prepared as possible for every interview situation. You just may find your opportunity.

CHAPTER 7

DISCOURAGEMENT AT A JOB FAIR

June 10

I went to my first job fair in 2000, while I was still in business school. A job fair sounds festive; I think of cotton candy, rides, and carnival barkers. When the economy was hot and employers were receptive, that's how it felt. Walking through a job fair was like walking down the midway—corporate recruiters leaned out from their booths to lure me with toys and chances to win a Palm Pilot or laptop. They all wanted my résumé. "Be sure to call me when you graduate," they'd say. It was fun to be desired.

Last month, I got an email about another job fair. Of the more than forty recruiting companies, most were pharmaceuticals and a few were information-technology consulting firms. After months of trying to get people to take my calls and respond to my letters and emails, access to a room full of recruiters seemed like an excellent use of time and energy. I was craving face time.

And this job fair was different. Participants would be screened and selected to interview with recruiters on the spot, I was told. If I emailed my résumé and made the cut, I would receive a confirmation number within forty-eight hours. A day and a half had passed when I received another email. I'd been accepted. I thought for a moment that perhaps the screening business was a gimmick to boost attendance; then I chided myself for my cynicism. Why would they do that? In a buyer's market, it made sense to screen to get the most appropriate people. The email explained that I'd need to bring paper résumés because the interviewers would not have access to my résumé on site. I made plenty of copies on good paper.

On the day of the event, which ran from 11 A.M. to 5 P.M., I wanted to arrive early. Beat the rush and see recruiters while they're fresh. From a list of participating companies, I selected the one I was most interested in and planned to target it first. When I pulled into the hotel parking lot at 10 A.M., it was already difficult to find a spot. In the large lobby of the hotel, the line to enter the job fair was already the length of a football field. I took my place at the end. As people continued to arrive, some walked past me and disappeared. Apparently, the line for those who had not preregistered was much shorter than the one for those who had. This unfairness caused those around me to start getting crabby. And it was only 10:15 A.M.

By 11:20 A.M., they were really crabby. We hadn't moved an inch in more than an hour. Rumors would occasionally drift back from the front of the line. Apparently the organizers had some problems. At 11:25 A.M., they gave up trying to do whatever it was they were trying to do. The line began to move quickly. They collected our confirmation emails as we moved toward the doors of the exhibit hall.

As I entered the room, I watched the other job hunters. Some were walk-running like children at a swimming pool as they tried to find their target companies; others stood still, looking around. I could see the horrible moment of realization on people's faces. Some understood immediately; others tried to cling to their hope and illusions. Eventually it struck me: There would be no interviews with recruiters. There was no plan and no order. This was a free-for-all. We were preselected to be chumps.

ANXIETY AND BODY HEAT

I worked my way to the end of a line for a large pharmaceutical company. I had applied for several jobs at this company through its website, to no avail. I wanted to understand what went on behind the scenes. The room—full of anxious bodies—was getting hot. The woman in front of me turned around and shot a suspicious look at me, perhaps wondering if I was standing within her zone of personal space by choice or by circumstance. I turned around and smiled at a large man behind me who was sweating profusely. "I just want to know which companies are hiring fat people," he said.

Finally, I reached a recruiter. I asked him how résumés were processed. "For each job posted we get a hundred to a hundred and fifty per day for the first few weeks," he explained. His advice was to apply for lots of jobs. That way, your application will be fresh, and someone might eventually notice you.

A desperate woman nearby was trying to get another recruiter to look at her résumé. "I don't want that," the recruiter told her. "If you give me paper, it will take three weeks to scan it into the system. It's better for you if you go to our website, look at the open jobs, and submit your résumé online." I wondered how long it would take for the recruiter to scan the résumé with her eyes.

I collected my wits and set off to find my target—an IT consulting firm. I was able to talk immediately with a recruiter because I was one of the first to arrive at her table. She looked at my résumé, said it looked great, and thanked me. She said they could use someone like me and that they'd keep me in mind. She seemed impressed with the research I had done on her company. I asked her if she had any questions for me. She said no, and that she'd be in touch. That's it. Mission accomplished. I was free to wander at a leisurely pace. It was now 11:35 A.M.

As I turned away from the table and back to the room, I saw that it had filled up considerably. In fact, I could no longer see any open space. Standing shoulder to shoulder, hopeful job seekers had formed lines to reach the various company tables. It was like Walt Disney World at Christmas—without the security and order imposed by stanchions and ropes. At least at Disney, you know you're eventually going to get somewhere and that the wait will be worth it.

CONSOLATION PRIZES?

As I drifted away from the table, I began to notice job seekers grabbing freebies and tchotchkes. What poor taste, I thought. That's like going to a business function and eating or drinking too much.

I looked for another line to join. As the room continued to fill, confusion built as lines intertwined. Seekers began accusing those simply trying to get around the room of trying to cut in line. "Is this the line for Merck?" "No. It's for Bayer." "Sorry! My mistake. Excuse me. Pardon me." The room got hotter; people got sweatier.

I found a table with no line. "You must be lonely," I said to the recruiter. She smiled. We chatted for a few minutes while I read her literature. She was trying to fill a single Ph.D. position in West Virginia. "Well, I have absolutely nothing to offer you," I said. We continued to chat. When I left, she wished me luck. "I hope you find the perfect job!"

I squeezed my way through a door into a lobby to get some air as someone was shouting, "Women and children first!" In the lobby, a line of new arrivals waiting to get in extended as far as the eye could see. This was futile. Should I just leave? No. I wasn't about to quit while everyone else was still working hard to make something happen.

Back in the exhibit hall, I discovered that I could learn more by listening to job seekers talking with recruiters than by waiting in line for a turn myself. "We're just here to point people to our website." "You might want to try our website." "I don't know what positions we have open, but if you'll go to our website . . . ". On and on it went at table after table. For the one rube in the room who had never heard of the Internet, I'm sure it was revelatory. But I had already been to the websites and had submitted résumé after résumé into the sucking black hole.

That's when it hit me. The job seekers grabbing the freebies and tchotchkes —they weren't crass, they were brilliant! These freebies were all that any of us would take home that day. I began to grab. From Wyeth, I got a bottle of ibuprofen. Ah, sweet success! I eyed dental floss on the Johnson & Johnson table. As I made my way around the line, I could feel the eyes burning into my back. Was I cutting in line to talk to a recruiter? Did I have some special connection or knowledge? Once I passed the recruiters, I dropped off the radar of those in line, and grabbed my waxed mint floss. I'd had enough. I was satisfied.

Walking though the hotel lobby to the exit, I saw the end of the line of those still waiting to get in. I walked up to it and addressed five or six people. "You're at the end of a very long line. I've just come from inside. Is there anything you'd like to know?" They were perplexed. "It's hot, crowded, and they'll mostly tell you to go to their websites," I explained. A woman at the end of the line looked at me with pity. She understood my plight, but she was different. "I have a confirmation number," she explained. "I was preselected."

THE JOB FAIR IS MORE LIKE A CIRCUS

One lesson to be learned from Tim's job-fair experience: keep your expectations aligned with reality. When unemployment is high, at a career event job seekers are bound to outnumber recruiters. The scene that Tim describes isn't all that uncommon when employers are in the driver's seat. Another lesson from Tim's experience: it's important to diversify your job hunt and try a mix of search techniques. Job fairs are just one method. And, for most job hunters, not a very effective one.

Despite this fact, job fairs are a staple for employers and job seekers alike. A survey by CareerJournal.com and the Society for Human Resources Management found that 70 percent of employers and 76 percent of professional-level job seekers say they use them. However, just 23 percent of both job seekers and employers say they're effective. Not a ringing endorsement. But the uninitiated still keep going to job fairs, and many meet disappointment:

I hate job fairs. I find them extremely upsetting in the current economy. The worst thing I saw was a job fair charging people to send their résumés to all the participants. Taking advantage of the mostly unemployed—how low. The second worst thing I actually experienced was a person who handed back my résumé. In my career, I have had that happen twice. It's hard on the self-esteem.

Long lines, few employers, lots of booths filled with irrelevant stuff like "California Highway Patrol is hiring" (not my career path), "M.B.A. programs" (already got one, thanks), "ITT Institute" (already have a bachelor's in electronics). Any interesting jobs get tons of résumés. The food and parking are expensive. That has been my experience.

Two things I get out of job fairs: OK premiums (giveaways) and sometimes inside info on a company from the human-resources person. —Ray R.

The job fair that Tim described is very similar to one I experienced a few years ago—except that it was being held by only one company. You could attend only by "invitation." After this experience I no longer go to job fairs.

I guess the real question on the table is why companies are holding these job fairs at all, especially if the only feedback or advice that is provided is to apply online. From my observation, the only things the events do is waste people's valuable time and create unneeded travel expenses. —Alfredo C.

The truth is that some job fairs are useful to some job hunters. They're a good bet for sales professionals—especially those in retail, insurance, and financial services. College seniors and M.B.A. candidates have success at on-campus events. Technical professionals are more likely to be disappointed. (A survey by Techies.com found that only 5 percent of tech professionals rated job fairs as the best resource for finding a job and most rated job fairs a 2.9 on a scale of 1 to 5, with 1 being "not effective" and 5 "extremely effective.")

Events organized specifically for your industry or field are far more likely to yield results. The most common ones are for marketing and sales, information technology, and finance. Avoid events in venues that are sure to attract the thundering herds, such as New York City's Madison Square Garden. And Tim's experience is a cautionary tale about "prescreened" events that seem to have taken a page from the Publisher's Clearinghouse Sweepstakes marketing plan: "You may already be a winner!" Here, the old saw applies: if it sounds too good to be true, it probably is.

ADVICE FOR THE UNDETERRED

If you think that, despite Tim's account, attending a recruiting event could be worthwhile, how can you make sure you get the most out of it? For starters, be choosy about the gatherings you attend so you don't waste valuable job-search time:

I just attended a job fair in Atlanta that had no traditional jobs with salary and benefits. It featured only straight-commission jobs and franchise opportunities. So if you find yourself at a job fair that isn't crowded or a cattle call, that may be the reason. —M.C.

The best way to find out about job fairs in your area is by reading the help-wanted sections of local newspapers. To find job fairs in your industry or field, check out the following websites, which carry listings of events across the country in a variety of industries and fields:

- American Job Fairs, Inc.   www.americanjobfairs.com
- CFG Inc.   www.cfg-inc.com
- HRLive   www.hrlive.com
- Jobhunt.org   www.job-hunt.org/fairs.shtml

Most announcements include a list of companies that will be present, so be sure to learn enough about the business they're in and the kinds of employment they offer. You'll want to make the most of your face time with recruiters.

Spend only about ten minutes at each booth. Some recruiters may ask you to interview on the spot. Ask the recruiter about the next steps in the recruitment process. And take the advice of this job seeker who said she was pleasantly surprised by the reception recruiters gave her at a job fair she attended, having expected a "'meat market' like those freshman mixers of yore" after reading Tim's account. She wrote:

It seemed like there were mostly financial-adviser and sales jobs at this financial-services-themed event. However, I did leave my résumé and make a two-minute pitch regarding my experience as a "one-person marketing-and-communications department, who can bring those skills to a communications team" with easily fifteen companies, including some big-name Wall Street firms.

I collected names or business cards from each person I met. Plus, I gave everyone I talked with a wrapped hard candy, saying, "This will give you some energy on a long day." Always find a way to be memorable—that's my motto. When I contact them again, to jog their memory I'll ask if they enjoyed the candy. —Janet F.

But remember, in periods of high unemployment, recruiters will be swamped, and it will be tough for them to recall you from among the hundreds of applicants they've met. So take the advice of this reader:

I just went to a job fair, and it was exactly as Tim described. Be realistic with your expectations—low! —Dave L.

And don't forget to take the opportunity to network with other attendees while waiting in line to speak to recruiters. It's possible you might meet someone who can help you with your job search, so never underestimate the element of serendipity in networking.

OTHER HELPFUL ORGANIZED JOB-SEARCH EVENTS

There are other organized job-search events that will get you out of the house and in front of people who can help you find employment. As previously stated, networking is by far the most effective way to a new job. Local job clubs, chambers of commerce, and other area business groups regularly host events that can put you in touch with people who have connections to employers. One of the best networking forums can be a luncheon, seminar, or other meeting of the nearest chapter of your trade or industry association. Consider the advice of this discussion-board participant:

Don't waste your time going to job fairs; they are too depressing. You need to spend your time around people who have jobs. They are the ones who are most likely to know about jobs. Do a search to find trade associations that might be appropriate to the job you want. Then go to their meetings and, if they are good groups, join. Don't bring résumés, but do bring business cards, and don't look and sound like a peddler. You can always send the résumé later. —Robert H.

JOB-SEARCH NETWORKS

You also may want to consider joining a job-search network. These organizations differ as to the services they provide. In some groups, members exchange tips on actual job leads they uncover, hoping that they can help themselves by helping others. In addition to providing unpublished leads, many hold monthly networking meetings, usually featuring a speaker, information about the job market, or guidance on job-search techniques. Some groups offer training, computer access, and other resources. They can be local or national in scope.

Members may be executives, managers, and professionals from a range of backgrounds, including business, industry, education, government, and nonprofits. Some groups, such as ExecuNet, limit membership to those earning more than a certain amount annually.

Other groups are tailored to a specific field, such as the Financial Executives Networking Group, Marketing Executives Networking Group, or the Human Resources Network. Some of the larger general-membership organizations include WIND (Wednesday Is Networking Day) and Forty Plus. Membership fees vary; they may range from about $220 for six months to $400 for a year. Decide which group or groups are appropriate for your needs and whether you can afford their dues.

HOW TO NETWORK AT GROUP EVENTS

For some people, networking is as natural as breathing. Then there's the rest of us. If you're among those who are uncomfortable at networking events, consider these tips for working a room with greater ease and better results.

First, prepare before the event. Find out who will be there and do a little research on their background and organization. Ask yourself: "What do I want to happen there?" Knowing what you want to accomplish helps justify your attendance. Your "elevator" speech will come in handy, so practice what you're going to say. But don't forget that listening is just as important as talking when it comes to establishing good relationships.

When you first enter a networking event, head to the bar for—preferably—a nonalcoholic beverage, then walk around and seek out a group to join. (Remember, you aren't attending to drink or eat, so do so in moderation.) Be careful to observe boundaries, and don't crowd into a group uninvited. One great networking strategy is to "pretend" you're the host. Make sure other attendees are having a good time. If you see someone standing alone, go up and start a conversation. Don't worry if you don't have the gift of gab. There's nothing wrong with an icebreaker like, "Large turnout, isn't it?" Ask plenty of questions, but never ask what they do; you may get the response, "What do I do about what?"

Gardner Heidrick, a founder of the search firm Heidrick & Struggles, once said, "The moment you ask someone what they do, they're going to turn around and ask what you do. And you may not want them to do that." Another executive recruiter says he never reveals what he does for a living at social events because he is invariably asked for job-search assistance. Instead, he says he's a consultant.

To have a pleasant social conversation, steer the conversation toward topics having to do with leisure, recreation, or neutral subjects. Good questions to start the ball rolling include these:

- "How do you know the host (or hostess)?"
- "Tell me about your children."
- "How did you meet your spouse?"
- "What do you do in your free time?"
- "Where are you from?"
- "How did you come to live here?"
- "Do you like to travel?"
- "Have you been anywhere interesting lately?"
- "Can you recommend a good place to eat downtown before going to a movie?"

Don't corner people you've just met for advice. They don't want to be put on the spot or engage in an anguished strategy session with you. If you want to talk with them in more detail, say, "I'd like to get your thoughts on my situation. Would it be all right to call you next week?"

Stay only as long as it feels comfortable. When you think it's time to go, be sure to shake hands and say goodbye to your host and key contacts. Outside, take a deep breath and say to yourself, "That went well." Phone or send a thank-you note after an event if it seems appropriate.

When you follow up with contacts, take care not to make it a full-court press. You don't want to seem as though you are badgering them for employment. It's OK to ask for job leads, but a networking call shouldn't feel like a sales transaction. Keep the stakes low. A direct but friendly approach works best.

WHERE TO SEEK MORE HELP

There are many other services available to job seekers. Indeed, in recent years career management has grown into its own industry, and the ranks of career counselors and coaches have surged. It might seem like a good idea to hire someone to "fix" your job-search problem, especially if you've endured a lengthy stretch of unemployment. However, no matter who you hire and how many pointers you receive, the bulk of the work will be up to you.

You can learn many job-search techniques by reviewing books or websites. A quick search online or a look at the careers shelf at a local library or bookstore will give you more information and advice than you could possibly use—all of it available free or at low cost. Of course, it takes discipline and stamina to apply all that knowledge. And you could be in need of support, troubleshooting, or just a sounding board. This is where a career counselor or coach can be valuable. If you decide on this route, you can find assistance through the Association of Career Professionals International (www.acpinternational.org) or the International Coach Federation (www.coachfederation.org).

If you decide to hire a career counselor or coach, be prepared to follow the suggestions you're given. It's common to hear these professionals complain that their clients only use them for gripe sessions and never actually get moving. If you pay for the advice, take it. Otherwise, you can't expect it to work.

CAREER-MARKETING SCAMS

While there's a place for bona fide career advisers, job seekers should beware of job-search scams. Steer clear of career-placement services that promise, for a four-figure fee or more, to give you access to the "hidden job market." Whether they call themselves retail-outplacement or career-marketing firms, these entities prey on vulnerable job seekers by using a variety of pitches. Some even present the illusion that you're among the lucky few selected to receive their help. Legitimate career counselors typically charge hourly fees on a pay-as-you-go basis; the shady outfits, however, usually require payment in advance of $2,000 to $30,000 or more. They may offer résumé preparation and mailing, counseling in interviewing and negotiating, and employment databases, but they often promise much more—specifically, entrée to jobs unknown to the public.

Unfortunately, some managers and professionals delude themselves, believing that they can hire someone to conduct their job search just as they'd pay an accountant to do their taxes. Many dissatisfied clients of these firms contend they could have done a better job on their own than the career marketers did. So before you sign a hefty check for assistance, consult with the Better Business Bureau (www.bbb.org) or Rip-off Report (www.ripoffreport.com) to see if any prior complaints have been made against the organization. Many change names frequently, so be sure to ask career-placement   services for customer references. Consider it a red flag if none are forthcoming.

THERE ARE NO EASY SOLUTIONS FOR JOB HUNTERS

The bottom line is that you must take charge of your own career. A job search requires a lot of legwork, and no one else can do it for you. To be sure, it can be a lonely endeavor. You'll experience lots of highs and lows, so expect those moments of discouragement or euphoria. During a buyer's job market—when employers have the upper hand—the going will be tougher than when candidates can call the shots.

● ● ●

Whether it's a "prescreened" job fair or job-search assistance, job hunters clearly must approach each new search strategy with their eyes wide open. There are no secrets or magic formulas to finding a new job. It's mostly just hard work. The most successful candidates approach their search as they would a full-time job and dedicate themselves to it on a nine-to-five basis.

CHAPTER 8

SERIOUS UNEASE SETS IN AFTER YOU'VE HIT THE WALL

- When Nothing You Do Is Working
- Helpful Comments Are Sometimes Hurtful
- How to Fight Off Depression
- Seeking Counseling
- Troubleshooting Your Job-Search Problems
- Making Needed Repairs
- Improving Your Outlook
- Networking Even More
- Taking Advantage of the Time Off
- Making Your Own Fortune

July 21

Well, I've done it. I've "hit the wall." I've reached a point in my job search where I don't have much new to try anymore. Do more of the same, I've concluded, just try to ride it out.

I've been unemployed for almost seven months. When I first heard about people who were out of work for twelve or eighteen months or more, I couldn't help thinking that maybe *they* were the problem. When we moved into my in-laws' house six months ago, I thought we'd probably be here for one or two months. I've been wearing the same three shirts ever since. Maybe it's time to get more clothes out of storage.

I continue to skim advice columns and books and am tempted periodically to try some new "technique." I try a few little changes here and there—a new cover letter, a new phone approach—but I'm unable to discern from the resultant data that these methods work better than the others I've been using. I'm playing more of a volume game these days, which is either desperate or brilliant. A couple of months ago I used to spend up to a day crafting a job-specific résumé and cover letter after thoroughly researching a company. Now I have three or four cover letters and résumés that I personalize with contact-management software and send to various employers at the rate of three or four per day. I do seem to be getting more responses—usually rejection letters. The quality of the rejections seems to be improving; now they're more effusive—for example, "I was very, very, very impressed with your credentials."

Extended unemployment has its difficulties as well. I'm sometimes concerned about overstaying our welcome at my in-laws'. They'd never agree, of course. But occasionally, when we eat dinner together, I feel tense. Maybe it's the heat wave, which has made everyone in New Jersey a bit crabby. Perhaps it's my own fear that I'll never work again, which occasionally bubbles to the surface when I'm tired or temporarily lose hope.

As I look at the stubs on my unemployment checks, I know this benefit is due to run out soon. I think the payments end in August, but I could try to get them extended. Of course, I could simply call the unemployment office and ask how to get an extension, but I don't want to just yet. I don't really want to know when the payments stop. I also have this fear that I'll call, and the clerk will say, "You haven't found a job yet? What's wrong with you?" The call will also lead to an audit, where the office will call everyone I've sent a

résumé to and verify that I applied for work. Each of the prospective employers then says, "You mean he hasn't found a job yet? What's wrong with him?"
While this nightmarish scenario probably belongs in a *Twilight Zone*
episode, it does cause me to wonder whether I really have done all I could.

THE UPSIDE

While I can think it's my technique that keeps me from landing a job, it's
equally easy for me to read *The Wall Street Journal* every morning and tell
myself, "It's the economy, stupid." With each executive arrest, bankruptcy
filing, earnings restatement, and Dow Jones drop, I find myself taking stock
of all that's good about being unemployed.

I'm thrilled to have spent all this time with my wife and daughter. We've lived
many years of weekend adventures together during these past months.
We've been to zoos and museums, parks and fairs, mountains and lakes. I've
been an integral part of my daughter's daily life for the past seven of her
seventeen months. I understand all of her vocabulary. She expects to see me
when she wakes up, at every meal, and at bedtime. If I'm not around, she
asks for me. When I pick her up at day care, I can watch her interact with the
other kids until she sees me and lights up

My wife and I have grown closer, too. We've worked through some difficult
issues that we might have sublimated for years had we been apart every day.
We're a stronger family for it, and I love her more because of it.

I'm ecstatic about some of the jobs that I didn't get. There were quite a few
that I didn't feel right about. I couldn't say exactly what was wrong with
them, which means that I might not have been able to justify turning them
down. For example, there was a privately held company that creates assessments to match people to jobs. The interview went well, and everyone was
very friendly, but I somehow picked up signals that the owners, a family,
were tyrants. There was a bit of a *Stepford Wives* quality about their nice-
ness. That, plus my potential supervisor's "zero tolerance for errors," had
me praying that they wouldn't call me back.

As long as I don't have a job, the excitement of the unknown remains. Where
will we end up? How will it all work out? Somewhere there's a job I'll
absolutely love. Each day I'll solve challenging problems at a rapid pace. I'll
contribute to making lives better for many people. That job will be so ener-
gizing that I'll feel guilty taking money for doing it. But I'll tell myself that we

have to have money to live, so we'll take it. It will pay a ton, so we'll be donating much of it to charity. So great will my passion for that job be that I'll return to my family members each afternoon (perhaps early evening) full of love and energy and the ability to nurture them.

Until that job comes along, I'm enjoying my totally flexible schedule. I'm wearing shorts and sneakers. I'm seeing movies in the afternoon. I'm sending out résumés. I'm wondering if I'll ever work again.

WHEN NOTHING YOU DO IS WORKING

At some point in your search, it's likely that you, too, will hit the wall. Nothing is happening, even though you're doing everything you can think of or have been told to do. You're sending out well-crafted letters, personalized to each employer. You use the Internet efficiently and effectively and don't linger too long online. You keep records of every company and person you've contacted and you follow up diligently. You continue to do research on employers and find names of networking contacts. But your phone doesn't ring, your email box is empty, and the mail carrier isn't even bringing rejection letters.

Has it occurred to you that this phenomenon, while unbelievably frustrating and discouraging, is more the rule than the exception? Nowadays, those who find jobs quickly and easily, without much angst, are rarities. The typical job hunter is a battle-scarred warrior who has spent weeks and months in the trenches:

Today marks five months without work and I don't have any prospects. I am at my wit's end and very much discouraged. It wouldn't be that bad if I were an unskilled person, since I would understand how the lack of an education would limit my options. But I have a background in information technology, with more than twenty years of service. I have even had my résumé reviewed and critiqued—yet no one calls. What is a person to do? I am at a point where I am seriously considering leaving this field. It has been very shaky over the last few years, and this is my third bout of unemployment in four years. It stinks. —Saxon L.

At this point, you have more options than you realize. Yes, you can kick the dog, yell at the kids, and wander along to the neighborhood tavern to drown your sorrows. Or you can take a philosophical and practical approach that starts by accepting the truism: this, too, shall pass. In the meantime, here are some practical steps for getting through this phase, from dealing with well-meaning friends and family members to troubleshooting the cause of your slowdown.

HELPFUL COMMENTS ARE SOMETIMES HURTFUL

Tim admits that he once assumed that a job hunter had to be doing something wrong if he or she was still looking for work after a year or more. Now he knows better, of course. But you may be picking up similar vibes from friends and family, who, while trying to help, are inadvertently making matters worse with their comments.

Though I know so many well-wishers and get loads of advice (as you say, everyone's an expert), I hadn't come across anyone who really understood what I am going through or knew how to express it—until I read your articles. I appreciate what my network of friends and colleagues is trying to do: show support, keep my chin up, give me hope, and help me with a game plan. But in the end, they often make me feel down when I am trying so hard not to get discouraged. Your articles helped me feel "connected" and made me feel a bit more at ease with the situation —RJ

I'd say the thing that makes me feel awkward is when people seem bewildered that I haven't found a job yet. Never mind the economic downturn this country is in, never mind that thousands of people have been laid off in my city along with the country, never mind that there are too many qualified people for too few jobs. They still give me the impression that I must not be trying hard enough. And sometimes I can't help but take that personally. I've done everything that Tim has done, short of the job fair (now I have to go because I want to see this spectacle for myself!) and somehow people don't think I've done enough. That's a little hurtful. —Lauriean U.

To address such comments, start by assuming that anyone who asks about your search is genuinely interested, even if what they say is a little oafish. If you assume someone is well-meaning, you'll have a positive attitude about them, which will reflect well in your answers.

If you're asked about your search, frame a response that revolves around what you're looking for, not why you haven't found it.

You: "I'm glad you asked me about my search. It's going quite well. At this point, it's important for me to find the right opportunity, in a place where I really fit. I'm laying the groundwork to find something that will be rewarding on a deeper level."

Them: "But you left XYZ company in August. How long is this going to take?"

You: "This type of thing is a process. I've had time for personal assessment and to explore new and different directions. I have some leads in the works, and I'm confident the right thing will come along. Your interest is great, though. Could I call you next week to discuss my situation?"

HOW TO FIGHT OFF DEPRESSION

It's easy to get down in the dumps and to beat up on yourself when you've been unemployed a long time. Once negative thoughts about your unemployment start rolling, they can pick up steam. Within a few minutes, you may find yourself believing you can't do anything right or that you're a failure. A good way to block this process is to reprogram your thought process—in essence, to "change the channel" to a more positive station in your mind.

The following comment posted on the discussion group shows how negative thoughts can feed into each other:

I have been unemployed for eight months now. I have an M.B.A. from supposedly one of the top programs and five years of management-consulting experience at a reputable firm, combined with an engineering background. After trying virtually every trick in the book I have resigned myself to never finding any kind of job that will allow me to afford a home or even a family. I didn't get here quickly, but the constant rejection eventually saps your self-confidence. Then the depression invariably sets in as you watch your savings being depleted day by day and realize that at some point, you will not be able to make rent. I don't really look for work, as there hardly seems to be any point anymore. Guess I am fortunate in that I have enough savings to support myself for five months before I will need to tap my retirement savings. Still, I spend a lot of time wondering how I got myself into this position and how I was stupid enough to ever buy the BS about the American dream.
—Ex Corporate Guy

To avoid succumbing to the blues, it helps to have friends to call for a reality check. They can tell you that such feelings are normal and to be expected, and then remind you of what you've accomplished and the good things you have going for you in your life. Often you can assemble a group of supporters from people you meet at local job-hunter support-group meetings (as stated previously, the Calendar of Career Events on CareerJournal.com has a national listing of such groups).

When you experience a downward spiral in your thinking, another good technique is to insert positive affirmations about yourself in your thought processes. These might include telling yourself:

- The national economic situation (or the slump in my industry) isn't my fault. The nation is going through a recession and employers are shedding jobs, not hiring. It's naturally going to take longer for me to find a new role.
- Job hunting is a numbers game. All I need is one "yes." I don't know how many employers I have to contact to find the right one, but I won't find it if I give up now.
- The fact that I haven't found a job doesn't mean that other areas of my life aren't going well or that I'm not a likable or good person. I have made wise decisions in the past and will continue to do so.
- Nothing about a job search is personal. I haven't talked with anyone long enough for them to like or dislike me. If I'm rejected or not getting results, it's because there are no openings or I need to change my search approach.
- Life is not unbearably rotten just because I don't have a job. Other things remain the same. I can still enjoy nature, the outdoors, spending time with friends and family, and participating in my hobbies—if I allow myself to.

Some people give themselves permission to feel sorry for themselves for a period of time. They watch movies, take naps, read, or ask loved ones to allow them to "whine" for a while. Indulging their emotions instead of denying them allows them to feel better. When the allotted time is up, they stop pouting and go back to the task at hand.

SEEKING COUNSELING

If you are unable to banish negative thoughts, feel tired and worn out for no apparent reason, lose interest in your hobbies or socializing, or show other signs of depression, you may want to seek help from a mental-health professional. Talking with a professional about your situation and gaining perspective on it may be all you require to spring back. A therapist can decide whether your condition warrants longer-term treatment.

Some community, religious, or government mental-health organizations offer subsidized counseling. Job hunters with restricted budgets may be able to make payments for their sessions to such agencies on a sliding scale, whereby fees are adjusted according to income levels. The following are good sources for finding a counselor:

- Referrals from physician
- Recommendations from trusted friends
- Crisis hotlines
- Community mental-health agencies
- Local United Way information and referral services
- Hospitals
- Government social services
- Child protective services
- Schools, colleges, and universities
- Referrals from clergy
- Employee assistance programs (EAPs)
- Emergency services (police, fire, rescue)
- Yellow pages

You also can look up counselors in your area via the online referral service offered by the National Board of Certified Counselors (www.nbcc.org).

TROUBLESHOOTING YOUR JOB-SEARCH PROBLEMS

Counselors say as many as three-fourths of all job hunters hit the wall eventually. Job searches usually break down at different stages. Some job hunters can't get job leads. Others land interviews but no offers. The reasons why are as varied as the job hunters themselves, who usually can't objectively analyze what's causing them to stall. Some have poor attitudes that spill over into their conversations with employers. Depression is a common problem, particularly among job seekers who lack a support group and spend much of their time alone. Other common reasons for stalling include the following:

- **Lack of Focus:** Instead of determining a specific goal, these job seekers apply for anything that's available. Employers nowadays hire only candidates who meet their exact needs, so it pays to apply only for openings that match your goals and credentials.

- **Poor Self-Marketing Skills:** Marketing requires finding customers who want your product and then creating materials and a presentation that positions it as the solution to a problem. But many job seekers believe they'll get hired on the basis of what they've done previously, not on what they can help an employer achieve in the future.

- **Inability to Network:** It's essential to talk with people who might have information that could lead you closer to employment. However, many job hunters don't understand how to network or won't do it because they fear they'll seem needy.

- **Lack of Structure:** Finding a job requires accomplishing a series of interim goals, but many job hunters whose searches have stalled haven't created a structure that prompts them to complete these activities. Others spend too much time on the Internet or doing busywork when they should be contacting individuals personally.

MAKING NEEDED REPAIRS

Seek help as soon as you realize you've stalled. That way, you can fix what you're inadvertently doing wrong without causing further damage. First, analyze what's holding you back. This usually can't be done on your own; you need to talk with colleagues, members of job-search support groups, advisers at a college career center, or a career counselor who can impartially review your approach.

Show your advisers your résumé and tell them what you've done so far. Together, you should pinpoint where your search is stalling and work first on fixing that problem. For instance, perhaps you don't hear from employers after sending your résumé for jobs you would fit. In this case, it could be that your résumé isn't serving you well. If you land interviews, but no offers, you may need to improve your interview skills.

As job seeker Bruce M. told the discussion group:

After almost a year of what seems to be fruitless searching, I have come to realize that my search has to take a new direction. If something isn't working, try to fix it or try a different approach. In short, I just stopped looking outward and have begun to look inward. Have you done this as well? Have you taken a long look at yourself and the things you love to do? Forget all the degrees and certifications. Concentrate on what you truly love to do and perhaps it will all come together for you.

I've tried to simplify what makes me tick, what I love to do, what I think I'm good at, what comes easy to me, etc. With these thoughts in mind, I then refocus my networking and job search. Alas, I haven't found the perfect match yet, but my frame of mind is much more positive and it makes the search so much easier. Also, the pleasant surprises along the way make the days exciting.

CREATE STRUCTURE FOR YOURSELF

Set weekly goals and develop a plan for reaching them. Do the difficult tasks first and reward yourself when you accomplish them with enjoyable activities, such as going to a movie with a friend. Your sense of well-being will improve as you reach these goals.

- **Act on the Suggestions You Receive from Advisers:** After determining your focus, prepare a résumé that targets these goals. Ask your advisers for feedback on your marketing documents. Research companies and hiring managers who are appropriate to your job target and approach them directly. Some candidates find that writing a personal letter, then following up with a phone call, is easiest.

- **Spend the Majority of Your Time on the Most Productive Tasks:** Limit your Internet activity to a maximum of about 15 to 20 percent of your search time, since the competition is greatest for jobs posted on the Internet. Contacting hiring managers personally increases your prospects because fewer people are likely to do so. To ensure you don't stay on the Internet too long, set a timer for your allotted time period and when it goes off, turn off the computer.

IMPROVING YOUR OUTLOOK

Make time during the week for activities that will improve your mental outlook and give you a sense of accomplishment. Here are some worthwhile pastimes:

- **Raise Your Brain Chemistry:** Physical activity helps improve mental well-being, so start exercising or going for walks if you aren't already doing so. Be sure to schedule time to be with friends and family, or simply spend time with a pet. Above all, don't stay cooped up in a home office for eight hours daily. Some candidates have trained for and run marathons during their unemployment.

- **Join a Job-Search Group or Form One Yourself:** Create a group of advisers for yourself. Seek feedback on your progress and be available to give advice to others. You may gain valuable information and insights. Moreover, being around other people is an antidote to the blues.

- **Volunteer:** Helping others or working on a cause you care about can help you feel more upbeat. One job hunter who was out of work for eighteen months always worked as a volunteer with his state's highway patrol on Friday evenings. He told his counselor it was "the one night of the week when I feel like a productive human being." Volunteering offers other benefits: you'll meet people who might want to assist you with job hunting.

At the eight-month mark in her search, Lauriean D. told the discussion group:

I try to keep my spirits up by working out a couple of times a week (hey, I don't have health insurance anymore, so I have to keep healthy!) and volunteering for a homelessness program twice a week. It helps me feel useful and appreciated, not to mention that it gives me perspective.

Susan W. decided after six months that "unemployment is quite isolating" and she needed to make a change. She planned to start volunteering "just to get out of the house and make a contribution somewhere."

- **Become Active in a Professional Group:** By doing so, you'll feel a sense of mission and accomplishment, make excellent contacts, and possibly get on an employer's radar screen, says marketing and communications professional Janet F. She writes:

My suggestion is to get involved with a local trade or professional association. Find a way to meet people at their events, make a contribution to their programs, or write for the newsletter. That way, people have a sense of what you could do for their department or company because they have seen you in action.

- **Accomplish Something Worthwhile:** If you're feeling like you have no control over events, choose an activity or task you've been meaning to do and finish it. The chore needn't be related to your career or job hunting. It could be as simple as cleaning out a closet or painting a room. The mere act of accomplishing something will make you feel better about yourself and more in control. As one job seeker told the discussion board: "My garden has never looked so good!"

- **Try Temping:** If you are running out of funds or need to feel stimulated professionally, signing on with an executive or professional staffing firm may be a good option. You can "test-drive" companies (while they in turn observe you), find out about internal job postings, and perhaps make helpful contacts. Some discussion group participants offered suggestions based on their temp experiences:

For me, a temp job has been a lifesaver. It helps get me up and out of the house in the morning, plus I am with other people. As you are probably aware, doing a job search can be a lonely experience as you are sitting at your home-office desk, making phone calls, and sending out résumés. An important thing is to be really organized so that the temp job doesn't become a procrastination tool for working at finding your real job. It certainly helps to pay the bills, too, so there is one less thing to worry about. —Nancy L.

It gets you into the ground level of a company (offering a few more possible contacts), and at least when you get home, you know you've earned something, regardless of how little. I'm temping right now, not in my field of choice, but since I'm simply filling in, I have a lot of free time to look for and apply to jobs (and the Internet connection is faster than my home one). Many people I know are doing the same thing. Also, I'm signed up with a few different agencies giving me more choices. Try smaller, local agencies. They know the area market and seem to work harder for you. —Jessica B.

NETWORKING EVEN MORE

By now, you may feel there's no one left to contact about your job search, but it's likely that you've only scratched the surface. This is the time to redouble your efforts to find new people to talk with. Even though you'd probably prefer to draw the blinds and isolate yourself, try to attend every suitable social or professional event you can.

Have business cards printed and ready to distribute so you won't be embarrassed when someone says, "I'll give you a call. Do you have a card?" It should include your name, address, phone number, and email address. This is a simple way to appear professional and businesslike. And it goes without saying that you are your own walking advertisement. Always dress well and don't smoke or drink excessively at gatherings. Poor personal habits likely will keep you from being referred to others.

Not knowing anyone at a social or professional event can be helpful because you won't have to deal with questions about your status. Your goal is to meet and chat with lots of people without seeming panicked, disgruntled, or depressed. You want to appear friendly, calm, and assured—in short, as someone who would fit the culture and values of a respected organization.

People with good social skills have the advantage. The best way to be interesting to others is to be interested in them. Everyone loves to talk about themselves; if you can get someone to do that, you have a shot at creating a conversation and a relationship with him or her.

TAKING ADVANTAGE OF THE TIME OFF

After they're reemployed, many job seekers look back on their stretch of unemployment and wish they had been able to enjoy the time more. Marketing executive Dave D. was laid off for the second time in three years in 2002, this time from a job he didn't like:

As I've told people, "The good news is that I've been through this before and know what to expect. The bad news is that I've been through this before and know what to expect."

I'm doing much better this time around, trying to enjoy my time off. The first time was shock, leaving a job I loved. This time it's relief, leaving one I hated. It's a spiritual adventure as well. I am thankful for so many things, and have had more time to notice the blessings.

If you can look upon unemployment as an opportunity, you may be able to do things you've yearned to do for a long time. For instance, sign up for a night course you've wanted to take through a local college or community learning program; explore local walking trails; learn French cooking or how to sew; or simply spend time with people you normally don't get to see.

Being at home during the day allows you to participate in the household in ways you normally can't—from picking up the kids after school to coaching sports teams to spending time in classrooms. You may enjoy making dinners or being available during the day to help neighbors.

I have used my time to learn more about myself and what I want to do with my life, so to speak. I have come to the conclusion that I think I would like a telecommuting job. Being at home is allowing me to spend time on papers for my M.B.A. I figure that God has arranged it for me to have time off from work, so I try to use it wisely. —Martha C.

Perhaps you'll find you're needed in ways you didn't expect.

As it turns out, my grandmother had a very bad fall after I turned in my notice and there was about a week between the time that she was released from the hospital and the time there was an opening at a nursing home nearby. She has since taken a few more turns for the worse, and she is now generally unresponsive. My father and uncles have planned just about everything for her funeral except the date. Everyone says that everything happens for a reason. I think the time that I have had to actually take care of her in her beloved home and the time I've had to tell her that I love her before she passes on and while she still understood me has been reason enough [to know] that I did the right thing in leaving my job. I think these times exist to remind us that we are more than what we do. —K. D. B.

MAKING YOUR OWN FORTUNE

If your search stalls and you feel a sense of hopelessness, remember, the right contact or company could be just around the corner. One discussion group participant relayed this tale:

A man walked miles over a barren desert. After wandering in circles for too long, he decided to give up and sat down to die. He was found on the other side of a sand dune just a few yards from an oasis filled with fruit trees and plenty of water.

● ● ●

Don't give up when your efforts seem fruitless. Take a few days off if necessary to recharge your batteries. Work on pinpointing any problems in your approach and then renew your efforts. It would be a shame to stop just when you may be on the verge of getting that call you've been waiting for.

CHAPTER 9

FINDING
THE SILVER LINING
TO A HUSBAND'S JOB HUNT

- The Difficult Role of a Spouse

- Expect a Range of Feelings

- So, How Do You Feel?

- Keep the Lines Open

- Dealing with Financial Fears

- How to Help When You Feel Helpless

- Talking with Children

- Finding Supportive Friends

- Ways Extended Family Can Help

- The Benefits of Unemployment

Tim often mentioned his wife, Claire Rosenson, as he chronicled his search. We asked her to give us her side to complete the picture. Her account follows.

First reactions tell you a lot about your inner state. Would it surprise you to know that when I first learned my husband had been laid off, my first reaction was overwhelming relief?

I know it's a terrible faux pas in the business world to speak critically of your previous jobs. After all, you don't want to sound like sour grapes. However, I've never heard of any rule against your spouse bitching about your former job, so here goes: Tim came home from that job every day feeling defeated, squashed. His former employer didn't seem to value creativity and straightforwardness and—absolutely fatal for Tim—humor was actually discouraged. I listened and observed, and only about six weeks after Tim started that job, I suggested he begin looking for a new one.

But Tim saw it differently: He felt a certain loyalty; he didn't want to be labeled a job-hopper; he wanted to accomplish something before he left. He agreed that the company wasn't a good place for him long-term, but his timetable was different from mine. I saw how unhappy he was and wanted him to start job hunting immediately. He wanted to wait "at least a year or two."

But I also had selfish reasons for wanting him to quit. It isn't easy to live in Boston on one-and-a-half nonprofit-job paychecks. I felt trapped in an overpriced, tiny apartment. My "office" was a tiny, cluttered desk crammed so tightly into a corner of the bedroom that I had to squeeze sideways into my desk chair. We hadn't put down roots in Boston and had no family there. I was ready to go.

THE NEWS BRINGS RELIEF

And so, may God forgive me, when Tim called from work that day last January and said "You'd better sit down," I was sort of hoping . . . Tim seemed to feel relieved, too. We reassured each other that we'd be all right. Our little daughter wouldn't be living on the street. We'd look back on this and be glad. It would be stretching things to say that the layoff saved our marriage, but I can say that with the question of when to leave taken out of our hands, a big source of tension was removed and we were both looking at the future in the same way.

Of course, it only took a couple of days for fear to set in: What if we couldn't get out of our lease? What if it took Tim a year—or more, in this economy—to find a new job? How long before the money ran out? In typical female fashion, I plunged into a pit of self-recrimination. I should be able to carry the burden for my family through this tough time, I told myself. I should be earning enough so that we wouldn't have to worry. Just a few years earlier, I'd been through a grueling job search with my freshly minted Ph.D. in hand. What I learned then was that, even in the best economy, a doctorate in the social sciences is actually a barrier to employment (long story—some other time). Now, when I really wanted to step in and become the breadwinner, those feelings of disappointment and regret came up again. If only I hadn't gone to grad school . . . if only I had a "real" job . . . if only I . . . if only. . . .

A few weeks after Tim was laid off, after landlord hassles and a flurry of negotiations with my boss, student-loan agencies, and unemployment offices in two states, as well as a stomach flu that knocked out each of us in turn, we arrived with an ungraceful plop on my dad and stepmom's doorstep in Princeton.

I am humbled and deeply moved by their gracious willingness to open their home to us. We took over half of the house and turned their dining room into an office. I did my editing and translating there—books and dictionaries in obscure languages all over the dining table and floor—and Tim set up Job-Search Central on the credenza.

INVADING THE FOLKS

Amazingly, my folks seemed to genuinely welcome the intrusion (invasion, more like). Naturally, little Hannah was the star. She learned to walk by careening from kitchen to dining room to living room to foyer to kitchen. She loved "helping" Grandma in the garden. She played with Grandpa on the screened-in porch. She greeted them both each morning as though they were her long lost best friends. What grandparent wouldn't be kvelling?

Tim seemed to thrive in this environment as well. My folks cheered his every success and agonized over his disappointments. They eagerly awaited his return from each interview, and their questions were insightful and helpful. Above all, they were encouraging; they had unshakeable faith in Tim's skills and abilities. I know that Tim felt nurtured, and beyond that, he just enjoyed their company. As for me . . . well, I felt both loved and grateful. But, let's face it, in your parents' home, you're always a child in some respects. It's just the nature of things. I found myself withdrawing a bit from the interview postmortems and other conversations, and I wasn't sure why. It was only later that I realized that I'd felt somewhat displaced from my role as Tim's helpmate and counselor (though this was never my folks' intention) .

When Tim told me that CareerJournal.com was interested in tracking his job search, I was against it. I was afraid it might distract him from his search and take away from our family time. Besides, I'm basically an introverted Internet-o-phobe. But this was about Tim, not about me, and he wanted to do it. And I began to see that the writing process was helpful to him in some ways—like therapeutic journaling. An added benefit was that it was something we could work on together. I felt good about helping him focus and organize his thoughts.

EMOTIONAL PATTERNS DEVELOP

And so the months passed in relative domestic bliss. We developed patterns: when Tim was feeling fearful, I'd be feeling positive and hopeful about the future, then we'd switch. This kept us from despairing at the same time. This may be some type of psychological mechanism that keeps couples from falling apart during difficult times. And there was the pre-interview/post-interview emotional cycle: Tim would thoroughly research every company before applying. He'd be excited, talking about what he could do for the organization. Then, when he was called for an interview, he'd suddenly declare he wasn't right for the job, he wouldn't want it if offered, it probably wasn't even worth his going, and so on. My folks and I gently teased him about these sudden, predictable attacks of the wobblies. At this point in the cycle, I felt he really needed my support. Fortunately, I believe my husband is exceptionally creative and talented, so building him up is no burden.

I'm somewhat surprised by one side effect of his layoff: as Tim tells me about his day, I find myself listening for bad news. I'm a little fearful when he tells me about his problems. I feel strangely relieved when I hear about positive feedback he's received. Tim says there's nothing to worry about, and I believe him. But perhaps I no longer believe in job security.

THE DIFFICULT ROLE OF A SPOUSE

Spouses and other partners of job hunters have a difficult role. While you aren't out there networking and interviewing, you bear many of the same fears and stresses, but largely as an observer who is expected to be more of a support "giver" than a "taker." Face it, how can you complain about your problems when your mate is jobless and must do battle daily with the corporate hiring gods?

Yet little has been written about spouses and what they can do to cope with their partner's job loss and subsequent employment. Claire's preceding account of her feelings during Tim's search sheds light on some of the difficult issues they face. It's time to give partners the recognition they deserve: It's a lousy job but someone's got to do it. Spouses and significant others, this one's for you. If your partner's job hunt is lengthy, you can expect to experience an immense amount of pressure, unwanted feelings, and family stress. The payoff, however, can be significant.

EXPECT A RANGE OF FEELINGS

In this day and age, relief seems an odd response to a spouse's layoff. Economic and global issues make unemployment scarier and more challenging than ever for many people. But Claire's reaction to Tim's firing tells us how stressful his last days and weeks in his former job really were. Many unemployed people admit, in hindsight, that they hated their former positions but held on to avoid searching for a new one or having to decide what they'd really rather do.

Claire's response also speaks volumes about the stress *she* was experiencing. For the spouses of someone who's unhappy at work, life isn't easy. The working partner's frustrations and uncertainty usually spill over into the family arena in some manner. These mates may eat too much, drink too much, exercise too much, yell too much, or do other things to extreme to avoid their own feelings or making a decision.

When employees know their jobs will be eliminated "at some future date," their firing looms like a ticking time bomb —the explosion is coming, no one knows when, and the waiting is unbearable. When the ax falls, at least the question is settled.

It's sometimes said that the uncertainty that precedes a decision is often harder than the decision; that waiting for an event is sometimes more difficult than the event itself. After a job loss, relief comes because the threat is over, the former reasons for misery have ended, and the unemployed partner can begin to take action. Even the littlest family members know the dreaded "thing" they anticipated has arrived and will feel relief. Tackling a problem is in itself a welcome exercise.

SO, HOW DO YOU FEEL?

Claire was honest enough to "tell it like it is" when giving her side of the story. She admitted being glad about Tim's job loss and ready to move on to the next phase. But she experienced her own emotional roller-coaster during his job search, which, fortunately, tended to move in the opposite direction from Tim's moods.

Tim's references to Claire in many of his installments show just how much he valued and relied on her support. Sure, it's nice to be positive and supportive all the time, but you're only human. As a spouse, you will go through the same feelings of grief and loss as your partner. You have lost the security, the well-being, and perhaps the prestige that came from having your spouse working in a certain job at a certain company. As a person dealing with a major loss or change in social identity, you can expect to experience the grief stages identified by Elisabeth Kübler-Ross—denial, anger, bargaining, depression, and acceptance—sometimes in random order, sometimes repeatedly.

Don't block or try to suppress your feelings. They will only resurface until you finally process them. Don't pretend it's "business as usual," either, when a veritable tornado is whirling around you. At the same time, you may not want to act on your initial feelings (just because you'd like to create a scene at your spouse's former employer doesn't mean it's a good idea). Remember, because you feel a certain way now doesn't mean you'll continue to feel this way in the days and weeks to come. Time will help you to put things into perspective.

Most likely, your spouse is going through his or her own emotional overload; although you need to communicate with him or her about your feelings, it's important to do so responsibly. The last thing you need to do is unleash your fears and other negative emotions on your spouse. This won't help anything, and it may harm your relationship at this particularly trying time. Find a supportive friend, relative, or counselor to speak with until you regain your equilibrium.

Don't use self-destructive coping methods—shopping sprees, overeating, and the like—to calm yourself. Turn to positive and healthy habits. For instance, if you enjoy exercise, continue to work out, which will improve your feelings of well-being. Do this throughout your partner's job hunt. Take aerobic classes, walk the dog, swim laps at the Y, have coffee and talk with friends, or take a long soak in the bath. Find activities that keep you centered. It won't help anyone if you become unraveled because you haven't taken care of yourself.

KEEP THE LINES OPEN

We've advised against unleashing your fears and other negative emotions on your spouse; however, this doesn't mean you should give your spouse the silent treatment. Silence can easily be perceived as blame, anger, or disapproval and raise unnecessary fears. So what is the best way to talk with your unemployed mate about your feelings? You don't need to skirt stressful topics, but you should avoid the language of confrontation. Your relationship will likely grow stronger if you can talk things out during this time. Remember, the elephant sitting in the living room isn't going to go away just because you ignore it. You and your partner need to speak to each other in ways that encourage the other person to open up and want to keep sharing. Here are some suggestions on how to do this:

- **Put Yourself in Your Partner's Shoes:** How would you like to be treated? Most likely you would prefer it to be in a nonjudgmental way. Keep this in mind when talking with your mate. If you're tempted to make a judgmental statement—"You aren't putting enough time into your job search"—turn it into a question instead: "How many hours do you feel you can productively job hunt each day?" This way, you may get some truthful answers and the reasons behind them.

- **Don't Play the Blame Game:** Nowadays, economic forces, cost pressures, mergers, and reorganizations are the cause of most job losses. Your spouse likely wasn't responsible for this event and shouldn't be blamed for it.

- **Try Not to Personalize the Issue:** This isn't about you. Nor was it done "to" you. Try to be as objective as possible about what has happened. After all, this is only about a job. Tell yourself that it's a far better problem to have than some others you could have been hit with.

- **Think Solution, Not Problem:** Being supportive means accentuating the positive and looking forward. Remind your spouse of his or her accomplishments and successes. Take his or her side whenever possible. ("That employer was shortsighted in not hiring you! I'm sure you were the best candidate.") Don't bemoan losses due to the job hunt. ("We'll take some camping trips this summer and a longer vacation after you find a new position.") Unconditional support builds confidence; the more your spouse feels this from you, the faster he or she will find work.

- **Stay in the Present:** Right now, at this moment, everything is probably fine. You have some money to live on, a roof over your head, and food to eat. Tell yourself that life is made up of a series of moments and if you're OK in this one, you'll likely be just fine in the next one and the one after that. It's only when you dwell on past mishaps and future fears that you're likely to bog down in worry or depression.

DEALING WITH FINANCIAL FEARS

Now let's tackle one of those future fears: finances. Many a spouse worries that the family will go broke before the partner finds a new job. While this can happen, typically the job seeker finds work long before that point. As soon as possible, though, you as a couple should sit down and draw up a plan for handling your finances prudently during this period.

As suggested in chapters 1 and 5, you should create a budget that's workable at this stage of unemployment. Assess your situation and determine how many months you can survive financially without your spouse's income. This indicates the amount of time needed for him or her to land the "ideal" position and the point at which a less desirable job may have to be considered to pay the bills.

If you haven't done so already, discuss your values and feelings about your financial goals and practices. Perhaps you both believe a child's college fund is inviolate and shouldn't be touched. There may be other funds you can't access at this time because of withdrawal penalties. You may decide that, as a couple, you need an inexpensive date night occasionally during the transition—if so, budget for it.

Depending on the time allotment you jointly agree to for the search, the family may not need to make drastic financial moves, such as selling the house. But you will need to be vigilant about sticking to the budget and spending responsibly. Worry less about appearances and lifestyle and more about managing your money wisely.

If you remain fearful about money, tell yourself that few people experience steady linear growth in their finances throughout life. Periodic setbacks are the rule, not the exception. With large student loans to pay back, Tim and Claire moved in with her parents during his job hunt. Like them, you can rebuild again.

As Keith T. told the discussion group:

My girlfriend's father was very successful, and then his partner wiped him out completely! Now he's starting a business again with his son, and he is very happy because the entire family supports him, loves him, and is with him at home. The man hit rock bottom, and he is sure he will rebuild his fortune again. I am inspired by him and think of him and his family whenever I get frustrated.

Think through the worst that can possibly happen to your family. If funds get low, you may have to do any of the following:

- Start working if you aren't already doing so
- Eliminate purchases you took for granted
- Sell your house and rent temporarily
- Seek government aid, such as subsidized school-lunch programs
- Move in with relatives
- Borrow from family members
- Relocate to another area

None of these actions is life-threatening. Who knows what may come of them? A move to another area might, for instance, lead to better, unforeseen opportunities down the road.

If your partner has been avoiding discussing your finances, ask why and listen to the response. Don't be critical of his or her feelings. Feelings aren't right or wrong—they just are. Remind him or her you want to be a partner in this effort, including managing finances, and that by not knowing the situation, you may inadvertently spend more than is prudent at this time.

HOW TO HELP WHEN YOU FEEL HELPLESS

Watching a loved one during a lengthy job search is painful. Each day, rejection can take a little bit of the person's soul. You know this person has much to offer but simply can't find the right employer or opportunity. You want to be supportive, but what if you say the wrong thing? As one spouse told the discussion board:

Today is our anniversary; my husband has been out of work for more than a year. He is young (thirty-seven) and very talented. He is very smart, hard-working, and ethical. He is incredibly efficient and a good speaker. And he can't find work.

We are very lucky in that I have a good job so that while we are gradually sinking, we aren't selling T-shirts on eBay like some of the posters I have seen in chat areas.

For me, though, it is exhausting, too. I am in my first professional job and don't know if we will have to relocate. I don't know how much I should give to this job and community. I feel as though a part of my life is on hold. My husband has held up extraordinarily well, all things considered. But it is eating at all of us. The uncertainty. The fear. I think the one-year anniversary really got to us. This doesn't happen to people like us. But it did. And there is a certain element of feeling hopeless and helpless. —Karen K.

While you may inadvertently say the wrong thing, if it's done in a caring way, it's likely there's no harm done. But you can help, possibly more than you realize. Here's how:

- **Remember That It Isn't Your Job Hunt:** Take an interest in the search, but don't try to manage it. Let your spouse know you're truly interested in his or her progress. Resolve to not interfere. Don't offer an opinion unless you're asked and even then, try to give it in a positive way.

- **Be a Source of Strength:** Help your spouse take responsibility for his or her career and future. Being a victim is an insidious attitude that erodes personal power. So is expecting to be rescued. We have more power and control than we think, and it's likely you can find ways to point out in a sensitive way that nothing will happen in the search unless your spouse initiates it.

- **Don't Eliminate Options for Your Partner:** Allow him or her to interview for out-of-town jobs. The practice will strengthen your spouse's interviewing skills, and new possibilities may open up. It's even possible that for the right job, you may decide you want to relocate.

- **Keep Your "Honey-Do" List in Check:** Don't expect your unemployed spouse to do all the household chores just because he or she is home. You may want some long-awaited tasks to get done, but searching for work is a full-time activity and shouldn't be postponed or avoided. It isn't fair to expect a spouse to find a new position quickly *and* do the grocery shopping, carpooling, laundry, and so on.

- **Be Supportive:** Accept that your partner's way of doing things may not be your own. Everyone has his or her own process. You may not agree with your partner's, but criticizing won't help. Be selfish: your goal is for your mate to find a new job as quickly as possible and being supportive is the best way for you to achieve it.

Allowing her husband to do things in his own way has been difficult for Mary, a spouse who told the discussion board about her struggle during his two-year job hunt. A stay-at-home mom for twelve years, she needed to go back to work as a legal secretary after her husband exhausted his severance and unemployment benefits.

Before my return to work, we lived on our savings. We continue now and then to burn up even more of our savings when we have to supplement my income. I don't make enough to support our family of four. Our children are on a state-funded health-care program, and my husband and I have qualified for health care through the health department.

Finally, after my pushing for this, about a month ago, my husband began working a couple of times a week as a substitute teacher, but this is for extremely minimal pay. I feel my husband should try to connect with some temporary agencies or get another part-time job while he continues to job hunt. He disagrees and seems to feel that subbing a couple of times a week indefinitely is the way to go—until he finds a job. I feel we should set a goal date for finding a job. He feels that's too restrictive.

I feel a great deal of resentment toward him since so much time has passed since he has contributed to providing for our family. I feel that his priority should be to make money even if it means a job that's menial or entirely out of his realm, but he is stuck on proceeding only with the caliber of jobs he has had during his lifelong career. He's fifty now and he gets few interviews in the area where we live.

Each day I look at him, the resentment just builds more and more. We totally disagree on how this situation should be handled, and I see no light at the end of the (now over two/three-year-long) tunnel. Meanwhile, from his point of view, I'm being unreasonable and impatient. We just get angry with each other all the time.

Job seekers helped her to understand her husband's side of things. As "BKN" wrote:

Mary: First let me say I appreciate your dilemma, as each one of us is faced with the choice of remaining steadfast to our expertise or branching out to some other discipline. Your husband is fifty—I'm forty-nine and anticipate his mentality. You see, he is at the crossroads, being fifty and all, and if he makes a shift at this time it is more than likely a final step from which he will not be able to return. His rationale may include these facts, in which case you are faced with a lasting decision: should he opt out and never return, guaranteeing minimal income forever—or stay the course in hopes that a break will come, in which case you will be thankful he was persistent?

I might suggest that you reach deep into your faith and support him during these times. I can tell you there is no real guaranteed approach in this environment. Your vow included for better or worse—be everything you can be at this time by suggesting alternative approaches that help to diversify the search while maintaining his support for his experienced decision. When this phase passes, your bond and commitment will be reinforced and the two of you may emerge for "the better."

Pamela S. was more succinct:

Mary: Getting laid off in this economy is like being diagnosed with a terminal illness. Your husband needs all the support he can get.

TALKING WITH CHILDREN

Tim and Claire's daughter was too young to sense the family's predicament. But children not much older than Hannah can intuitively sense when things are not right—or merely different. First, Mom or Dad is home and available to play, make meals, or take them to school. Second, as much as you try to conceal problems, a mood change may be evident as well.

A generation ago, it was common to not tell children about "grown-up" problems. Today, experts don't recommend this practice. While children don't need to know the nitty-gritty details, it's wise to offer a simple and truthful explanation about what's happened. As a couple, you need to explain that one of you won't be working for a while but expects to find an even better job soon.

Naturally, explanations for elementary-school children will be couched differently than those for teens. Answer any questions that come up. Reassure your children that they will always be loved and cared for. Kids have a way of accepting news we feel is earth-shattering so long as they know their parents are OK and that they'll be OK as well. You may be surprised at what your kids tell you. With so many layoffs nowadays, they may have friends whose own parents have lost jobs.

Sons and daughters of all ages also like to feel they can help with a parent's cause. Tell your children about ways they can help. You'll likely need to ask your kids to not disturb you when you're working on your job search. If you need to start budgeting family funds, explain that you'd appreciate their help on this, for example, by renting movies free from the local library instead of from the video store or scaling down birthday celebrations temporarily. Every family has areas in which they can cut back; as a group, you can sit down and make a list together, then compliment everyone on the savings they generate.

Continue to communicate with your kids. If you notice that they seem anxious or their grades drop, or you hear that their behavior has changed at school, address the issue immediately. Children deal with their fears in unexpected ways. Schedule some inexpensive yet enjoyable family or one-on-one activities. Talk about the positive aspects of your unemployment, such as getting to spend more time with them or going to "dollar-movie" matinees on the spur of the moment. How you behave with them during this time will serve as a powerful lesson about how to deal with life's difficulties. As Karen K. told the group about her husband's unemployment:

I can tell you the upside. The time off has allowed him to be closer to my children and his stepchildren, and we all have really enjoyed that. The kids will miss having him at home when he does go back to work.

FINDING SUPPORTIVE FRIENDS

Many partners say that they learned who their "true friends" are during an employment transition. Don't be surprised if people you once socialized with now pull away. Friends may change the subject if it comes up or refuse to acknowledge it. This can bring up powerful feelings of rejection, shame, anger, and, no doubt, loneliness in you. At worst, you may feel you have some sort of infectious disease.

> It was a learning experience for me to find that the so-called "friends" whom I helped time and time again until they found a job (in some cases, one I found for them with a customer or other contact) won't even return your phone call when they know full well what happened to you and why you're looking. However, I believe there are still good and decent people around who can and will help—the trick is finding them among all the other "weeds." —Marketing Gal

Realize that while acceptance of unemployment has generally increased, many people don't know how to handle grief or trauma well. When a significant loss occurs for them or someone else, they feel awkward and self-conscious. By not mentioning the proverbial elephant in the living room, they think they are helping, when in reality, that's all you want to talk about.

If acquaintances pull away, realize it isn't your fault and don't hold it against them in the long run. For whatever reason, they simply aren't capable of offering encouragement, but you shouldn't burn bridges that can remain intact in the long run. Friendships can exist at all levels—from intimate to superficial. Each works as long as you keep it at that level. Don't force intimacy on people who don't want it—or lack the capacity to accommodate it.

By the same token, being around people who can't support you probably isn't good for you right now.

But perhaps you can't avoid certain people. You see them at church, school, and neighborhood gatherings. You can break the ice with such people by bringing up the subject first; for example: "You may have heard that John's employer reorganized and eliminated a number of positions. Unfortunately, he was affected. He could have stayed on in a lesser capacity, but he chose not to put his career on hold for a few years. So he's looking for a challenging opportunity, with his company's full support. I just wanted you to know this. We are disappointed his work with XYZ Co. is over, but we're looking forward to the future. We hope we can count on you for your support. Can we call you down the road and update you about his progress?"

You will likely find that many friends do stick by you, but be careful not to overload them with your feelings. Everyone has a limit to what they can absorb and how much support they can provide. As sensitive as your friends may be to the situation, continually hearing about it may get old. Choose your topics and limit how long you discuss them.

The good news is that people you may not know well may emerge from the woodwork to provide unexpected support. You may be surprised by just who steps forward to offer encouragement or a sympathetic shoulder. Such individuals may have been through the same thing before and know how you are feeling. They'll jump into the boat with you and help you row. These people truly are gifts in your life and may remain lifelong buddies.

Help your spouse by arranging casual social activities with people who accept you both for who you are, not for what type of work you do or did. It's not a good idea to withdraw from the world. Having pleasant evenings with enjoyable companions can take your minds off issues and lift your spirits; this, in turn, will help with the search effort.

WAYS EXTENDED FAMILY CAN HELP

Your own family or your in-laws can offer a range of support, from taking you in—à la Tim, Claire, and Hannah—to simply not making discouraging comments. Some relatives who've never worked or aren't familiar with situational cost-cutting may think your spouse is to blame for the job loss. Have a prepared statement ready to use when criticism or judgmental questions come up. The last thing your spouse needs is a meddling father- or mother-in-law.

Be sure to set up ground rules concerning the support you accept. If you receive a loan, be clear about the repayment rules. Does the loan include interest? When does it need to be repaid? What conditions are attached? No amount of aid is worth making compromises you can't tolerate or promises you can't—and shouldn't—keep.

If relatives offer to help, come up with concrete ways they can do so. A casserole prepared occasionally, an invitation to a barbecue or weekend home, or an afternoon of babysitting may be exactly what you need, especially if you have to return to work.

Networking assistance is always a welcome contribution. At some point, a relative may be able to provide a part-time job or a recommendation to an employer. Don't be afraid or embarrassed to ask. The worst you'll hear is "no" and why. In fact, if you don't ask them or provide specific suggestions on how relatives can help, they may feel useless—and stop offering.

THE BENEFITS OF UNEMPLOYMENT

For job seekers, it's difficult to recognize some of the long-term good that can come from unemployment. As a partner, you're in a unique position to help. Losing a job and looking for a new one can be a time for renewal and fresh starts. It can mean shedding a work persona that no longer fits and finding a position that meshes with new values and integrity. If your spouse wasn't happy in the position he or she lost, remind him or her of this; point out that finding the right role may bring a sense of peace and satisfaction to the family that wasn't there before.

Remind yourself that supporting your spouse is a selfish activity that will benefit you. You'll help the job seeker find work more quickly, and you'll improve your relationship. A true sense of partnership will prevail following this experience. You will have grown personally. You'll now know that you can be relied upon during times of difficulty. You will know how to give and receive support. Your spouse may not say as much, but he or she will appreciate you on a new level. As Karen K. says,

We are closer than ever. Maybe all marriages should face major challenges in their first year or so—to give them a real-world test.

Children can learn that obstacles can be faced with courage, perseverance, patience, and a sense of humor. A dramatic event in the family needn't kill its spirit. While families don't normally wish for a parent to be jobless, some report being better off for it. Children always want their parents around more and never see it as a bad thing. Help your spouse recognize that this time can be a gift. Find ways to fit in activities you wouldn't have done otherwise, while not interfering with the job search. Like Claire, you may say you wouldn't have traded the experience.

● ● ●

A family is a living organism; when one part is disturbed or unhappy, so is the whole. Your partner's job loss and subsequent search will affect you and your children in many ways. You'll manage the experience better if you know what to expect and how to provide constructive support.

CHAPTER 10

PASSION
IS THE SECRET TO
JOB-SEARCH SUCCESS

August 13

I'd run out of energy and ideas in my job search. What happened next? I got a second wind, which was really a fifteenth or fiftieth wind, except that this one was more pronounced than the many little highs and lows that preceded it. They were like cycling through Elisabeth Kübler-Ross's five stages of dying over and over at various intensity levels. But now I'm back in a big way.

Let me digress: a reader who posted a message on the discussion board says that it's passion that really sells, and that's what I needed to get a job. This advice brings to mind a quote by the French dramaturge Jean Giraudoux: "The secret of success is sincerity. Once you can fake that, you've got it made."

It's obvious that people want to hire people who are passionate about the work they're doing. What I didn't get until lately is that there's a difference between selling passion about something and just being passionate. It's a subtle difference: the first state requires effort, while the latter is effortless. It's the effortless version that people want, and you can't fake that, or even try to create it with the best of intentions. It's easy for me to forget this fact, because I keep feeling like I need to do something in order to get a job; I need to win over the interviewer.

Just wanting a damn job (a sentiment I've previously expressed) isn't enough to get the job. While I've gone into job interviews with every intention of becoming passionate about the job, I have not gone in being passionate. I've always wanted the interviewers to do at least a little bit of selling, too. I've needed them to convince me that I want to work for them. I have no doubt that many interviews in which the interviewee is acting passionate have resulted in successful employment. But the interviewer must feel better when the candidate is already doing and loving the job in his or her own mind.

My true passion lies in nonprofit and educational work. I've just had two interviews at a nonprofit organization that helped me remember what real passion about work looks like. I was surprised by this discovery. I didn't do anything different, yet I was different.

I've spent most of my life working for nonprofits large and small (and a few small for-profit businesses). Working to serve the noble missions of arts, human-services, and educational institutions was a part of my identity. (As an adolescent, I experienced a slight but omnipresent dread that I might end up as a brand manager for Frito-Lay. Why Frito-Lay? I have no idea, and I apologize to all the fine people who work there. It's just that it isn't right for me.) Yet I'd grown tired of the inefficiency and the lack of business acumen in so many that I'd encountered or worked with in some capacity in the non-profit world.

SIDETRACKED

Tempted by the lures of the for-profit world, I went to business school because I wanted to take for-profit business and management skills into the nonprofit arena. Most people in business school did not even understand what nonprofits are. ("Why would any business try to lose money?") I arrived at business school during the heady dot-com days. I was wary, but I felt the undeniable pull of dot-com lust—a quest for power and wealth in equal parts. It was a dizzy, gold-rush kind of intoxication. Though I couldn't see a viable business model, I thought it might be fantastic to work at one of those places with a nonsensical name. (My wife refers to them collectively as "FishWire.") I had a growing desire to make money and began to think that making lots of it was good. I grew to believe that my idealism was childish and naïve. I sometimes felt stupid for wanting to help people grow.

When I was laid off eight months ago, I decided to exclude nonprofits from my job search. I was fed up. I was ready to make a hop. I'd hoped that it would be to a large publicly held company. I thought that I could prove myself if I succeeded in the "big leagues." But I found it difficult to get passionate about maximizing shareholder value. And that missing element of passion has been evident in my interviews and applications.

I worked hard to cross over. Then came the tech-sector crash, the perp walks, and the painful, dirty disclosures and discoveries that have permeated and undermined the capital markets—the "greed on steroids," as Ralph Nader describes it. Not only was I disgusted, but the for-profit jobs I'd been seeking also became more and more scarce.

I started applying to nonprofits again, not out of passion or any kind of self-less desire; they had the jobs. Nonprofits in general weren't downsizing or rightsizing. And the more I talked with people involved in nonprofit work, the more I rediscovered my passion for it.

In my two recent interviews with a nonprofit, I was so impressed with the work the organization was doing that I wanted to meet with its managers just so I could share my appreciation. When the interviewers asked questions, I wasn't trying to figure out the right answer to get the job, I was trying to figure out the right answer. I felt an inner peace and humility because I wasn't trying to prove anything to anyone.

I got to that place, not by logic or as a result of thorough research, but through my heart. I didn't know any more about this job than about any other for which I had interviewed. I simply knew in my bones that I wanted to be involved with what these people are doing, whether or not I got a job. I was already an evangelist for them.

What I've just learned is that if I'm wondering whether I'm passionate about something, then I'm not. Would I take a job I wasn't passionate about? You bet I would. But I feel so much better when I'm passionate about what I'm doing. Can everyone have a job that they're passionate about? I doubt it, because there are a lot of lousy jobs out there. I hope that everyone can be passionate about something. And I know that passion about work is very important to me.

THE LINK BETWEEN PASSION AND SUCCESS

Tim's account of how he found his second wind when he rediscovered his passion holds a powerful message for job seekers. When you're doing something you love and find fulfilling, you know it. Employers know it, too. Hiring managers can sense the enthusiasm and energy that a candidate with career passion will bring to their workplace. And they can also sense its absence. A role you aren't in wholeheartedly will drain all your energy, and no employer wants to hire you for it. Even though you may desperately want "a damn job," as Tim puts it, you likely won't really want it after a couple of grinding weeks or months.

Having career passion is all about making a connection between your work and your heart. Discussion-board participants were eager to share their testimony on the subject; for example:

As the son of a lifelong fine artist who never really made it big, I have a close understanding of what passion is. As Tim suggests and my father very well knows, when you have a passion for something, you will likely do it for no pay at all—because it is what you need and want to do. Naturally, in our world, money is all-important, but there can be no greater happiness than when one can be truly passionate and earn a few dollars along the way! —J. T.

WHAT IS CAREER PASSION?

Social psychologist Abraham Maslow devised a "hierarchy of human needs," ranking our basic motivations in a pyramid model. Survival requirements, such as the need for food and shelter, are at the bottom. Next comes security, followed by social acceptance, then self-esteem. At the top is "self-actualization"— the full use and exploitation of one's talent, capacities, and potential. When you're fulfilling yourself and doing the best that you're capable of doing, you'll have found your true passion. It's important to our overall health and well-being that we love our work and find renewal and growth in what we do for a living. When you do what you love, your job becomes a vocation, whether it's putting together investment-banking deals, writing code, building bridges—you name it.

Some psychologists describe career passion as working in a "flow state": your work fascinates, stimulates, and engages you at such a level that you can easily lose track of time. Passion about your work will manifest itself in career success.

You'll spend most of your waking hours at work, so why not do something you love? This sentiment is often championed in the career-counseling field.

Yet, national statistics on career satisfaction show that 50 percent of all Americans would change careers if given half the chance. Some folks stay in jobs or professions they don't like because they don't know what type of work they'd prefer or don't want to take a step down in pay or prestige. Some stay out of fear of the unknown. They may believe, at some level, that they aren't competent and that they're lucky to be where they are. They may talk about starting new careers, but when given an opportunity to make a change, they give up their dream. And there are folks who think that searching for passion is a luxury best left for a strong job market.

Of course one can't be expected to be passionate about every facet of a job. A poll of employees would reveal that most people make tradeoffs, and most jobs are a mix of good and bad. How to find that perfect blend of passion and employment opportunity? Countless professionals struggle with this dilemma.

As a veteran job searcher—I've been "downsized" four times, and all the companies eventually failed, including my latest experience at a dot-bomb—I completely agree with Tim that passion is a critical element in a job search.

Unfortunately, not all of us have a passion, and some of us who do have one have difficulty translating it into something that an employer would hire us to do. For example, I grew up overseas and have a passion for travel, yet we all know that business travel is quite different from leisure travel. The one time I tried a job with a lot of international travel, I got burned out after a year and didn't want to travel in any capacity for a while.

I also have a passion for teaching. I did manage to figure that one out and become an adjunct professor at a local business school. But I wouldn't want to do it full time. I have a passion for sports and contemplated playing two different sports professionally, but, as with teaching, found that I couldn't dedicate my life exclusively, as one must these days, just to playing a sport.

I have a passion for relationships and mentoring others, but doing this is more a function of who you work with than what you do, so that doesn't necessarily lead you directly into an 'area' where you can work with passion.

Essentially, I agree with Tim that it is more important to be passionate generally than to have a passion for something. But either way, I think it is very difficult in our society to find a way to live out your passions in the workplace. —Peter S.

"WHAT DO I WANT TO DO WHEN I GROW UP?"

Following a layoff, it isn't uncommon for midcareer professionals to ask themselves this question. If you've been working in the same company for fifteen to twenty years or never had to look for a job before, it can be startling to realize that you can now do just about anything you want. You don't have to continue working in, say, insurance, or telecommunications, or wherever you've spent the majority of your career. If you're like most professionals, you have transferable skills and can choose from an array of options. The selection may be as overwhelming as when you were looking for your first job after college.

There's no better time to reevaluate your goals. (If you're like Tim, you may embark on a career switch, only to come to appreciate the one you have.)

It can trigger a rediscovery of who you are and your mission in life. But how do you figure out what your passion is?

Start by thinking of the best job, class, volunteer project, or other activity you ever had. For some people, this is an easy enough exercise. Think of a time when you were energized and engaged in your work: you couldn't wait for the day to start, staying late wasn't a problem, and you felt you made a difference. Author Kurt Sandholtz calls this your "career best." Find what makes this connection to your heart, and you've found your passion.

To think about it another way: if you were creating a "highlight film" of your career, what would you include? What do you remember fondly and why? There are many ways to approach this process of self-discovery. Inevitably, it's a meditative process. Consider the story of this job seeker and his advice:

So many people feel they have to accept jobs for what they are because they have to pay the bills, and they drag themselves off to work each day.

I left a stable job in April, with good pay and benefits—call me crazy— because it was turning me into a miserable person and stealing my happiness. After dabbling in some consulting, I've regained my happiness and learned more than ever what makes me "tick," what qualities, challenges, environment, and other attributes I'll seek in a job. It's cost me some money, but now I won't be going crazy and dragging myself to work like millions of others who don't look forward to waking up and who live for 5 P.M.

My advice for others: Take a moment to be true to yourself and understand what drives you and piques your passion. Write it down on paper and study it. It might mean some give-and-take, such as location or even pay, but you will be happier in the long run and hopefully the passion you bring to the job will lead to the promotions and compensation you want. Dreams are only dreams until you make them a reallly. —Sean R.

THE FREEDOM TO CHOOSE

Readers intuitively sensed that Tim's initial search for a position in the corporate sector wasn't right for him. Discussion-board participant Susan S. offered this counsel to Tim and posed three questions to test his commitment to his stated career goals— indeed, these are good questions for any job seeker to consider, no matter what sector he or she has chosen.

First, is working in the corporate world your passion? Or is it what you're "supposed to do?" You're young still. Wouldn't it be fantastic if you could answer this question now instead of when you're fifty?

Second, have you and your wife talked about making changes to your work lives that might give you both a bit more balance for your child and each other that will still pay the bills, not "a few little changes here and there," but invention, creation, and thinking outside the box? For example, starting from a clearing of possibility versus the tweaking, prodding, and pummeling that you've already done. We can pound our pillows into the shapes that we start out with at night, but, in the end, it's still the same old pillow we sleep on. Do you get the picture?

Last, you're not stupid or inept. You're just human, and a young man at that, bound by your and society's ideas about what a man is. It can be quite stifling, no? What would your life look like if you had the freedom to choose?

MEANING AND MISSION

When we are younger, we all have dreams, hopes, and aspirations. But often societal, emotional, and practical pressures push them aside. Fear, uncertainty, and self-doubt can wind up playing a greater role in career decision-making than they should. How can you once again tap into your inner passion?

- Listen to your intuition. Trust your inner voice when it tells you to act, then take the appropriate steps.
- Use creative visualization. Tap into your imagination to create a clear picture of what you wish to happen. Focus on this regularly until it becomes a reality.
- What do you do best now? What are your selling points? Think about your skills in terms of which might be transferable to a new career.
- Tell yourself: "I can remake my life." You have the power to reshape your destiny. If you're feeling unhappy and unfulfilled, you can choose to make a positive change.

While you can follow your passion in all types of work, whether in the nonprofit or for-profit sector, it's no surprise that Tim's story connected particularly with readers at nonprofits. Many professionals working in this field are seeking a greater sense of fulfillment from their work. And undoubtedly there's appeal in making a difference while making a living. His discussion of passion inspired a number of readers to write in to the message board:

I agree that passion is the key to a successful career. That is why people go into fields like teaching, firefighting, police work, and government. It's not for the money. I left the private sector for federal employment ten years ago and have never looked back. Federal employees get criticized from time to time, but the work I do is important and I have no regrets. —John N.

For some—not for all—it really is about passion. I've worked for fourteen years in the nonprofit sector and four years in corporate America. All have been in marketing, communications, and advertising, but not all have been happy. I recently left a large, well-known law firm to go to work for a children's hospital. I've found that at the end of my roughest days now, I go home satisfied. It means more to me that sick kids get well than that rich lawyers (even nice ones—and yes, there are plenty) get richer. You eventually learn what makes you tick, and it's a great lesson. —Leigh M.

The meaningful, mission-driven work that many nonprofit organizations offer can sound enticing to refugees from the for-profit world. For some, the gap in pay can be made up by the nonmonetary compensation of knowing their work has a positive impact on people's lives. Just don't be misled into thinking that working in a nonprofit is less demanding than working for a for-profit employer; nonprofits face their own set of stresses, with fundraising at the forefront.

Of course, following your passion doesn't have to mean working in the nonprofit sector, even if your dream job involves healthy doses of altruism. Many occupations offer the opportunity to make a difference in the world. For a listing and descriptions of hundreds of jobs, review the Bureau of Labor Statistics' "Occupational Outlook Handbook" (www.bls.gov/oco), which is updated every two years. And following your passion by no means requires toiling for a meager paycheck; many fulfilling jobs pay hefty salaries. As many well-to-do professionals can attest, success is an offshoot of passion, and money is often a byproduct of success.

VOLUNTEERING

Jobless professionals may want to consider volunteering during their stint of unemployment. Now, more than ever, there is a huge need for volunteers, with many charitable organizations struggling in the economic downturn as donations have plummeted. Volunteering is a good way to maintain your energy level during an extended job search. One discussion-group participant offered this suggestion based on her own experience:

With twenty years of corporate-marketing expertise in Los Angeles, I approach each day with a renewed sense of commitment to finding passion in my work once again. I need to approach my search with the same amount of passion, but admittedly some days are easier than others. I am looking at volunteering and using my marketing skills to make a difference while I continue down this path. —MaryJane T.

Volunteering offers several other benefits to job seekers. It can help to keep skills sharp and spirits up for developing new contacts and job leads. It can help you build additional skills—such as setting strategy and vision for an organization—which you may not otherwise get to do on a day-to-day basis in your professional role.

Knowing that you are doing something good for others is a great way to boost your self-esteem when you're feeling down. This increased self-confidence and satisfaction will show during interviews. It's a plus if your volunteer work can tap into your passion; it will be something positive to discuss with interviewers.

COMMUNICATING YOUR PASSION IN COVER LETTERS

Candidates who exhibit a combination of enthusiasm and self-assurance are irresistible to employers. Try to convey these qualities in your cover letters. Your résumé shows that you're qualified to do the job, so don't rehash the facts presented there in your letter. Instead, express directly and indirectly why you would enjoy working there each day, why you would be a good person to work with, and how you would exceed your manager's expectations. Here's how:

- Be clear about what the job requires. You can't demonstrate enthusiasm and commitment without thoroughly understanding what you'll be expected to do. Study the ad or job posting, talk with others in similar positions, or sleuth around until you locate an employee who can tell you about the opening.
- Know what problems you'd be expected to solve. When screening prospective candidates, what is the hiring manager hoping to fix in the short and long term? What are the critical issues involved? How can you address them?

- Understand your own goals, beliefs, and values. You can't be passionate about something unless you're sure what you stand for personally.
- Know what the company values. Compare it with your own beliefs. Determine where they overlap or diverge. For instance, if an employer places a high premium on honesty in all its dealings, a candidate for one of its openings could mention how important it has been to maintain personal integrity throughout his or her career.
- Think about what you'd like to know if you were hiring someone for this job. What would pique your interest and make you take notice?

Now you're ready to write. Keep your letter short; four paragraphs is long enough. Address your letter to the hiring manager or senior executive in charge of the department where you'd be working. Here's one format for conveying passion:

- In the first paragraph, mention your keen interest in the job and how you heard about it. If you were referred by a friend or found out about the position in an unusual way, mention it. Next, briefly describe the issues the company and hiring manager hope to address by filling the role and how you could solve them.
- Continue this train of thought in the second paragraph by briefly describing how you've dealt with similar issues in the past. Mention one or two representative problems you've overcome in prior roles, including the employer's name or type of business. Stress the excitement and triumph you felt in being able to help your employer deal with the issue. A problem-action-solution formula may be a useful way to tell this story; quantify the outcome if it is impressive and it illustrates your ability.
- In the third paragraph, state why you particularly want this job and why the company should hire you. Don't be afraid to brag about yourself. Describe what benefits the organization would receive from having you on board, while making your interest palpable. For instance, you could say, "For the past XX years, I've focused on developing and strengthening my abilities [in this area], to the point where I seldom [make a mistake, don't achieve the goal, don't meet 120% of expectations]. Since I first heard about Widget Co. [mention how] I have wanted to be a part of its team. I can promise that you would see an immediate improvement in [quality, profit, service] if I were hired."
- In the fourth paragraph, state that you would like to move to the next step in the hiring process and will contact the addressee if you don't hear from him or her first. Always follow through on this promise.

The resulting letter should speak personally to the hiring manager. If you feel your wording is too formal, imagine that you already know the individual you are writing to. Subtly suggest that you are already part of the organization, perhaps by sprinkling the word "we" into your sentences. And finally, before sending your letter, ask an excellent grammarian and speller to proofread it for errors. (For advice on writing cover letters in response to job postings, see chapter 11.)

SHOWING "FIRE IN THE BELLY" IN INTERVIEWS

There's no doubt that enthusiastic, congenial candidates do better in interviews than those who don't convey passion for the work. Building a rapport also is essential, and candidates can do so by showing good humor and genuine curiosity. Being invited to interview means the company believes you have the skills and background needed to perform the job. Beyond that, hiring managers want to determine if you'd be a good "cultural fit." You can demonstrate how well you'd match the environment and culture by how you dress, talk, and present yourself during the meeting.

Passion can be easily communicated in how you answer an interviewer's questions. If you love doing this type of work, don't hesitate to say so. Ditto if having a position like this has been a dream of yours. Surprise the hiring manager with your initiative by mentioning one or two critical challenges you would like to help address (this is where advance research comes into play). Think of ways to incorporate what you've learned about the employer's philosophy into your responses. For instance, you might be able to tie one of your personal values with one held by the company. Or perhaps you have a career goal that meshes with an organizational value.

Always be truthful, of course. There's a fine line between being sincere and being smarmy when interviewing. Your enthusiasm and passion will come through, but only so long as what you express is sincere.

● ● ●

Follow your heart, and you can't go wrong. When you enjoy your work, everything else can fall into place. To find a job you love, you can't start by looking at job postings. The first place to look is within yourself.

CHAPTER 11

COMING
FULL CIRCLE

- Finding the Right Match

- What Could Be Harder
  Than Job Hunting?

- Changing Your Search
  Direction Midstream

- Responding to Job Posting

- Confidence Comes from
  Knowing What You Want

September 6

I tried for most of seven months to find something in the for-profit world. And, having spent the major part of my work life in small enterprises, I dreamed of working in a large corporation. Because of the recession, though, there weren't many openings in the pillars of capitalism. To make matters worse, the narrow and specialized nature of the bulk of the available jobs made me fear that, should I win one, I would become a cog in some-one's machine. This conjured up visions of boredom, Huxley's *Brave New World,* and Orwell's *1984.* (What is a validation specialist, anyway? If you've been looking for work in the past year, you've seen these positions advertised.)

I'd spent a good portion of my career in the nonprofit sector. While my heart remained true to the social missions of nonprofits, my head had grown weary of working in environments where there was never enough money or staff to accomplish the stated goals. For seven months I'd refused to con-sider nonprofit work. But in a conspiracy between my eyes and my heart, my attention began to be drawn to the nonprofit classifieds masquerading under such headings as "health care" or "education" that I'd trained myself to skip over in *The Wall Street Journal* and *The New York Times.* They usually offered broader responsibilities than the for-profit jobs. After a family beach trip over the Fourth of July holiday and a much-needed respite from the job-search grind, I gave in. Since I wasn't getting anywhere in the for-profit world, I decided I should consider nonprofit jobs once again.

THINGS START TO CLICK

There are several good websites that specialize in nonprofit jobs. Once I started looking in that sector again, I incorporated these sites into my daily list of sites to search. For the first few weeks, I saw what I considered to be the predictable list of openings. Many of the positions had interesting titles that suggested close proximity to the action, but the salaries suggested that they were essentially volunteer positions. The jobs demanded lots of educa-tion and experience, and they offered great responsibility. But the great responsibility wasn't usually matched by great pay. As much as I love the nonprofit sector, I still can't figure out how a lawyer who has argued cases before the United States Supreme Court can afford to work for $28,000 a year unless he or she has already made a million. I'm not so fortunate. In short, I was depressed by most of what I saw. I craved the excitement and responsibility, but I also had to make a living. Since we've come to parenthood relatively late, my wife, Claire, and I have observed that its vicissitudes and associated humble lifestyle aren't quite as charming as they might be when you're in your twenties.

The first nonprofit jobs I applied for were throwaways: they paid so little that I couldn't possibly have taken them, but the exercise got me into a groove. After applying to five or so positions in the field I'd previously refused to even consider, I saw an ad that was really intriguing. The challenge was audacious and suitably "in your face." The scope of the work and size of the operation implied that the organization might actually be able to pay a living wage. While I can't remember the exact wording, the ad read something like this: "If you're ready to try something new, have diverse experience, are entrepreneurial, can operate in a highly decentralized system, and want to help grow a $100MM organization, give us a try. We're looking for a partner, not someone with all the answers. If you need your own office and a secretary, don't bother to apply." I loved the ad, and it made me laugh. I couldn't even tell what the job was, which suggested that the employer didn't know either. I was thrilled at the possibility that I might have the chance to define the job myself. (Validation specialists, I'm guessing, aren't offered the same flexibility.)

From the email response address, I found my way to the organization's website. I still couldn't figure out what it did, but I could tell it was big. I created a brutally honest cover letter in which I listed all my complaints about the inefficiency and incompetence I'd so often seen in nonprofit management. I explained that I wanted to help nonprofits run responsibly. I emailed the letter and my résumé, then I promptly forgot about it.

GOOD TIMING

About a month later, I got a call from the executive director's assistant. Claire took the message. The assistant wanted me to interview with the executive director and chief operating officer. When I called him back to schedule the interview, I asked as delicately as possible if he could send me some information—something—that would help me understand what the organization did.

The call had come at a good time; I'd had several interviews that week and was feeling good. I was also sufficiently busy that we couldn't find a mutually agreeable time to meet for about ten days, which allowed me time to think and research the organization.

The package, which arrived a couple of days later via FedEx, included an annual report of sorts and detailed financial information. That's when I began to understand the impressive scope of the organization's operations. I learned about its history. Its values, vision, and mission contained some of the most beautiful language I've ever read. The prose was deeply moving, yet simple and economical, like Lincoln's Gettysburg Address. While I was immediately cynical, I reasoned that if the organization lived even 10 percent of what it professed to espouse, I would be honored to work there.

So, after a spring and summer of trying to break into the corporate big time (or small time, depending on the particular opportunity), of trying to fall in love with positions I feared might stifle me, I was back where I'd started. I was falling for a nonprofit once again, despite my promises to myself that I wouldn't go back. I hoped that I could walk into this interview with my eyes wide open.

FINDING THE RIGHT MATCH

Many people become disenchanted with their chosen fields and yearn to enter another—and get paid for it! Tim certainly did. But every aspiring career changer should heed Tim's experience, because it illustrates the difficulty of making a significant professional change at midcareer. It also proves how important it is for those of us who start disliking our jobs to decide whether the career or the employer is to blame. This can eliminate a lot of unnecessary headaches.

For example, Tim never stopped loving the nonprofit world and the concept of "doing well by doing good." What he disliked was not being able to achieve important goals for his nonprofit employers due to a continual lack of funding. When he was laid off, he understandably tarred the entire not-for-profit arena with the same brush and decided to seek his fortune in the corporate world so he wouldn't feel as frustrated.

While Tim might have enjoyed working in corporate America for a while, it's likely that after the "honeymoon" of winning and starting a new job ended and he began to experience typical problems that arise in corporate bureaucracies, he would have remembered his former nonprofit employers more fondly. Yes, they often lack for funding, but they typically give employees a sense of meaning and mission.

WHAT COULD BE HARDER THAN JOB HUNTING?

So don't say we didn't warn you. Switching careers isn't easy, especially as you get older and more experienced in your initial field. The process takes more effort, time, and energy than a search for the same type of job you held previously. Before you begin, be clear about why you didn't like your former work. Try to isolate what you did from the environment in which you worked. Did the work itself make you happy? Could it be that the real culprits behind your dissatisfaction were your boss, coworkers, working conditions, hours, travel requirements, or other issues? Sometimes, taking a step back—as Tim was forced to do during his job hunt—and reevaluating what you're passionate about can clear up the issue for you.

Perhaps you truly don't like your industry or your function. In this case, you'll need to do a great deal of self-assessment and evaluation to find alternatives that take advantage of your innate and most enjoyable skills and abilities. The less dramatic the change you make, the easier it is to find new opportunities. For instance, you will likely find a new role faster if you remain in the same function and only switch industries—if you're, say, a marketing professional who wants to move from consumer products to pharmaceuticals—or if you stay in the same industry but switch to a related function; for example, moving from an engineering position to a marketing position with an electric utility.

In both instances, it's possible you'll already have contacts in the field or industry in which you're continuing. Because they know you, they can vouch for your work ethic and ability to learn quickly. Or they may be willing to take a chance on hiring you, despite your lack of experience in the new arena.

Many people, though, do decide to make a dramatic change in career path. Consider Paul A., a job hunter who chose to switch careers because he was unhappy in his former position. He made his decision after talking with friends about his seemingly innate abilities.

After a twenty-four-year career in business development and sales with IBM, I am changing careers into public relations. Although I am still unemployed—my search began at the end of June—I am confident I can land a PR job representing an issue in which I have an interest. Many people have told me that I should be in public relations since I am comfortable and skilled at meeting and introducing people.

Since Paul wants to change functions and industries, he has decided to make things easy on himself and do it as a two-step process. First, he plans to seek a sales role at a public relations firm. Once in the PR industry, he then hopes to become a PR practitioner. As defined earlier, this would mean first staying in the same functional role while changing industries, then staying in the industry and changing his functional role. Paul further expanded on his strategy:

My entrée into PR could be by leveraging my business-development and sales skills to assist PR practitioners in gaining clients while I learn the subtleties of PR.

Once you're sure you want to switch fields, expect to work harder than the average job hunter at finding opportunities and convincing employers that you're a good risk. Paul knows he faces an uphill battle to meet new contacts in the public relations field in the various industries he's targeting—but he's sure it's worth it:

To me, this is about more than money. This is my future and I want to be able to sleep at night knowing I accomplished something more than selling widgets. And this is also about a career—not about a job.

Here are some key steps you need to take to convince employers to hire you in a new field or sector.

- **Take Courses, Volunteer, or Moonlight:** Undertaking these kinds of activities in areas related to your desired new profession will demonstrate that you are sincere about wanting to make the change; they will also give you experience to list on your résumé.

- **Realize Your Change May Require a Sacrifice:** As an unproven risk, you may have to "pay your dues" in the new field and you may need to start a few rungs down the ladder or relocate. Naturally, your initial earnings may decline as well. When considering a career change, decide if this is a price you and your family are willing to pay.

- **Have a Convincing Reason for Wanting to Change Careers:** Interviewers will undoubtedly ask you why you want to make a career change at this point in your life. Your reply should be brief, articulate, and logical; for example:

"I originally was drawn to writing and public relations and took courses in this area in college. But the job market was slow when I got out of school, and I decided to try sales. At first, sales was very exciting but I always enjoyed preparing collateral materials more than other aspects of the job. It just wasn't my true calling, even though I was good at it. This transition has given me time to reflect, and I am confident that I would be more of an asset to an employer in public relations. My volunteer work in PR for the Metro Humane Society has really shown this to be the case. I realize that this change will set me back financially and that I may have to start at a lower level, but I am willing to make sacrifices in order to help companies communicate with their communities."

- **Know That Your Route to a New Job Is Networking:** When you're changing careers, you're not likely to hit paydirt by responding to advertisements in which the company seeks candidates who meet exact requirements. You need to convince decision makers to spend time on the phone or in person with you. This may require making hundreds of cold calls.

- **Write a Résumé That Links You to Your Career Goal:** A chronologically formatted résumé isn't much help to career changers, particularly when mailed in advance. In fact, it can even be a hindrance if it raises questions about your lack of experience in the new field or industry. You will need to construct a functional résumé and/or write marketing letters explaining the logic to this move and how you can provide tangible value to an employer. These documents should highlight any volunteer, committee, or peripheral experience related to your new goal.

CHANGING YOUR SEARCH DIRECTION MIDSTREAM

It's possible that after trying to change careers, you may realize, like Tim, that you want to stay in your original field. Don't be surprised by this about-face in your thinking. Sometimes it takes exploring new areas to know you aren't interested in them after all. To return to your former field, you don't have to return to Square One of your job search. However, you will need to revise your search tools and strategy. You'll need to reorient your résumé and cover letters to your new goal; target different employers; start reviewing Internet job sites in your prior field; make new networking overtures; attend meetings of your former professional association(s); and redouble your efforts. You still have momentum, but not as much as before.

As previously mentioned, it's also important to know why you grew disillusioned in your prior job, so you won't repeat this situation at the next company you join. If you become frustrated about not being able to achieve goals in large organizations, seek out opportunities in smaller firms. Look for managers with characteristics different from those of the manager who gave you migraines. Or seek a team environment if you don't like being a solo contribu-tor. You have the ability to control these and other factors affecting your job sat-isfaction at a new employer.

RESPONDING TO JOB POSTINGS

For Tim, accepting the wrong job was a more frightening prospect than being paid less than he was worth. So after he found his "real" passion and began once again to seek opportunities in the nonprofit world, he was surprised to spy an intriguing help-wanted advertisement almost immediately. The ad didn't tell him much about the organization, but he was able to track down its website and glean some information. He then composed a beguilingly honest letter that he hoped would separate him from the pack of other contenders.

Since Tim found the first job opening he could get passionate about in a classified ad, let's focus on how to respond to these ads. In truth, a relatively low percentage of senior-level people find work by responding to ads. Those who do typically meet the exact requirements specified in the advertisement or attract employers in other ways. Apparently, Tim sensed what this nonprofit wanted to see in candidates: honesty and out-of-the-box-thinking. How can your cover letters work as effectively? Here are some rules:

- **Try to Find Out More about the Employer:** If a name is provided, research the company and allude in the cover letter to something you've learned from your research. If the ad is "blind," or doesn't include the company's name, you may be able to track down the specifics from an email address or by calling the post office and asking for the name of the advertiser who used this particular P.O. box number. In some cases, you can locate the name of the top official in the department with the opening and respond directly to that person.

- **Always Include Your Correct Contact Information:** This may seem obvious, but recruiters are amazed by how many people neglect to include current (or even any!) addresses or phone numbers on their material. Include your street address, your home and cell-phone num-bers, and your email address.

- **Respond to the Requirements Listed in the Ad:** Don't bother to reply if you don't meet the basic requirements. Unless employment is so low that there's a dire shortage of applicants, companies will only seriously consider respondents who meet all or most of the requirements in the ad. If you are a good match, it might help to divide your letter into two columns. In one column, cite the requirements listed in the ad; in the other, cite your matching experience, point by point. If you can demonstrate that you match the employer's needs almost exactly, you have made a convincing case for being contacted.

- **Reply to the Tenor of the Ad:** If an employer only loosely defines a job, it may be more interested in seeking someone who will "fit" its culture and values. In this case, you need to be creative and respond to the issues raised "between the lines." In Tim's case, this meant showing his entrepreneurial side, his disinterest in superficial trappings and executive perks, and his passion for helping nonprofits become more efficient. Apparently Tim decided that an organization that didn't respect his honesty wasn't one he wanted to work for. His approach worked.

- **Present Yourself as a Solution:** Focus on the employer's interests, not your own. Stating what *you* want (e.g., "I'm seeking to use my skills in an environment where I can grow as a professional and be rewarded commensurately. . . .") rather than what the employer wants won't do much for your candidacy. On the basis of both the ad and your research findings, think about what the organization most wants and address that need. To repeat, companies don't hire people; they hire solutions.

CONFIDENCE COMES FROM KNOWING WHAT YOU WANT

Many job seekers say that things seem to click into place once they know in their gut what type of job they want and they take charge of their career. Think about it: if you are casting around in the wrong industry or field, nothing will really be a good match and you will appear desperate instead of confident. Your answers to interview queries will be forced or half-hearted and you won't have the enthusiasm that comes from really liking a position and company.

Once you are sure of yourself and your agony of indecision is over, you will have renewed energy and self-confidence. Your answers will come easily and you and the employer will seem more like collaborators on the same team than warring parties watchfully circling each other.

If you still aren't sure about your goal, pay attention to what feels right emotionally and physically as opposed to what you believe intellectually to be possible. Do you get a headache just thinking about what a particular job might entail? Does your stomach seem to be tied in knots? Our physical selves often can tell us things that our logical minds may prefer to overlook.

● ● ●

There is nothing worse than taking a job that isn't right for you. Even if it pays well and you like your coworkers, those factors won't be enough to make you happy. When you leave this position (and you will) and begin job hunting again, you may feel as though you've been thrown to the lions. Do yourself a favor and don't entertain offers for positions that aren't a good fit. It is better to keep job hunting until your ideal situation comes along.

SEALING THE DEAL

September 24

My interview was on a Thursday. I'd had several days to learn all I could about the organization, and I was eager to meet its people and see how they did what they did. I wasn't entirely sure I knew what they did; but their principles had struck a chord with me. I hoped I would be able to use both my head and my heart in the interview.

THE FIRST INTERVIEW

By the time the day of my interview came, I just wanted to meet these people and tell them how moved I was by their vision and its manifestations. They had created a model of nonprofit efficiency that I'd only envisioned. They let the visionaries control the programs, while they did the part that nonprofit founders are traditionally horrible at doing: running the business. But I wasn't desperate to work there. In fact, I wasn't even thinking about getting the job. I'd seen the organization as an object of beauty. I didn't need to possess it; I needed simply to admire it.

When I arrived, I was struck by the vastness of the central office. Laid out in a huge open floor plan, it looked like the *Washington Post* newsroom as depicted in the movie *All the President's Men.* Just desks and people as far as the eye could see. I saw people of all colors and ages in all styles of dress. This wasn't the standard corporate environment, and that was good.

I took an immediate liking to the chief operating officer and the executive director. They had many questions for me; the volume and variety were invigorating. In so many of my interviews at other organizations, I had supplied the only energy in the room; I'd had to entertain a bored, self-indulgent Roman emperor from human resources. In this room, we supplied energy equally. There were no airs and no games.

As they asked and I responded, we shifted into a dialogue. We were brainstorming together about some of their most challenging issues. We were in perfect flow. I felt like we'd been working together for a long time. Two hours quickly passed. I left refreshed and assured of a second interview.

Saturday night I received a voice message from the COO. She apologized for the short notice and wondered if I could attend a meeting on Monday. It was, she explained, a natural opportunity to meet the entire management team. After that, she'd like us to have lunch with the chief financial officer. I was a little troubled by a call on a Saturday night; were there appropriate boundaries between work and personal life? But I was also excited by her obvious enthusiasm about my candidacy. I left a message at her home on Sunday saying that I'd be delighted to meet with them the next morning.

THE SECOND INTERVIEW

When I arrived that Monday morning, I was ushered into the meeting room and seated at the end of a table with about fourteen expectant people already in attendance. They'd all reviewed my résumé. Though the questions came from all directions, I was amazed at how supportive everyone was. Usually in a group this large, at least one person has some evil agenda. That person doesn't want to hire me because he or she likes another candidate, is angry at the boss, or wants to spite so-and-so. There was none of that. After thirty minutes, everyone filed out of the room, each person shaking my hand. I was shown to a waiting area. The COO would come get me for lunch in a few minutes. While I waited, participants from the meeting approached to chat. I felt very welcomed. During those five minutes, somehow the COO also got feedback from everyone who had been in the meeting.

THE NEGOTIATION

The CFO joined us at the restaurant. She had some specific issues to discuss. She ate quickly and left for a meeting. The COO asked me if I was "terribly expensive."

"That depends on what you consider expensive," I replied.

"Well, that's fair. That puts it back on me," she said. "I want you to work with us." From that point, it was simply a matter of negotiating the details. We went a couple of rounds on salary. We talked about responsibilities. I suggested that the organization might need an information technology strategy plus other things. I could provide these and also serve as the COO's right hand. I didn't want to get pigeonholed in the IT spot. She liked this idea.

I knew I wanted to work with her and the organization. I asked for a couple of days to think things over. I took a day, and said I had hoped for a bit more money, but that I wanted to work for her. Her response: she didn't want me to start the job wondering if I'd made the right decision, so she sweetened the offer a bit more. I felt great: she'd heard me, and she cared.

HOW DO YOU KNOW IT'S THE RIGHT JOB?

Tim's description of his interviews with his prospective employer prompted one reader to remark that it "sounds like a fantasy"—and indeed it does. The search and hiring process is often described as a courtship: two people get acquainted, fall in love, and make a commitment to each other. To make a good match, both partners need to know what each wants from the relationship. Employers need to communicate their expectations—perhaps with a little prodding from the candidate—and feel confident a candidate can fulfill them. Meanwhile, candidates should know what they want and be sure the job will satisfy these needs and goals. When you're in a lengthy job search, it's tempting to disregard sensible advice and jump at just about any offer. The question that this reader posed to the discussion board is a common one:

I have received only one job offer, but it's for a position that I really don't want to take. Should I accept just because I don't have any other offers? —RC

Julius offered this counsel based on his own experience:

I also had an offer for a position that I thought was open to failure in this market and that I would basically hate. My advice is to hang in there as long as you can before making a mistake that makes your résumé look like Swiss cheese. I said no and have been getting other opportunities since.

As discussed in previous chapters, getting in touch with your dreams and hopes for the future while taking a hard look at your skills and accomplishments is as much a part of an effective job search as résumé writing and networking. The more focused your efforts, the more energy-efficient they will be.

Make an effort to examine the issues unemotionally. Consider all facets of the opportunity and identify exactly what's wrong with it. Do you dislike the interviewer, but like the company, the job, and the job content? If the position offers the role and the advancement you're seeking, it's worth reconsidering. Seek the perspective of a reasonably objective third party, such as a recruiter, an outplacement counselor, or a contact who works for the company.

Virginia M.B.'s comments, more practical in nature, are equally worthy of consideration:

Deciding if you should accept a job that you don't really want can be very difficult. There are several things one needs to consider:

- Is there severance pay—and for how long?
- Are you receiving unemployment benefits—and for how long?
- Do you have medical coverage—and for how long?
- Do you have a spouse with a good income and medical benefits?
- Is there enough money to meet the mortgage payment, utility bills, food, and other living expenses?

If you have more "no" answers than "yes" answers to the above, I would suggest that you take the position and keep looking. Who knows? Once you have the job, you might begin to like it, possibly improve and change it, and at the same time contribute to the organization's goals. Remember the old adage, "A bird in the hand is worth two in the bush."

If you still have trouble thinking clearly about your decision, try using an exercise devised by Benjamin Franklin, called "moral or prudential algebra." When facing a difficult decision, Mr. Franklin would divide a piece of paper into two columns labeled "Pro" and "Con." Then over the course of three or so days, he'd list the different reasons for and against the decision under the appropriate heading. After reviewing the list, he'd estimate each item's respective weight, and when items from either side would balance each other out, he'd strike them from the list. After a day's consideration, he'd have his answer.

Of course, given the financial and other pressures facing candidates, this type of exercise is easier said than done. The difficult part is determining the weighting each consideration deserves. Conduct this pro/con analysis with your "perfect job" criteria in mind, taking the long-term view. Don't give short shrift to quality-of-life issues, such as family considerations, stress level, and health concerns. Mr. Franklin's isn't a perfect system, but often there are no easy answers when it comes to making career decisions. Most likely you'll have to make some compromises. Just make sure that they're ones that you can live with.

ASSESSING CULTURE FIT

"Culture fit" is often cited as the number-one reason why new hires fail—so naturally, it's always a top concern in the interview process. Your prospective employer is deciding if your personality and background fits its culture. As a candidate, your goal is to find out if the organization's culture corresponds with your interests and values.

It was once common for interviewers to ask candidates to describe their ideal job. Given today's sophisticated interviewing techniques, such a question now might be viewed as a cliché and easily forgotten. But even before you start preparing for a specific interview, it's wise to ask yourself this question early on. Envision your ideal work situation, including the type of organization and supervisory style. You should be able to articulate what your next job will look like at a level of detail that goes beyond a generic statement.

To do this, you'll need to be true to yourself as well as honest with interviewers. Some job seekers told us they have difficulty with these basics:

It kills me not to be able to have a true and honest two-way conversation with a prospective employer. I pray for the day when I will find a prospective employer with whom I can be completely honest and not have it backfire or work to my disadvantage. —Fabienne P.

Lying or misrepresenting yourself is never a good idea in the hiring process. It will catch up with you. While a little fudging might help you over some hurdles, the whole picture of your candidacy is likely to emerge in the interview, and falsehoods are often discovered after employees are hired.

Of course, as Tim did, you'll want to do your homework: scrutinizing the organization's website and picking up on cues from the office environment and employees. Dig deep into the personality of an organization and how you'd fit in. Find out what kind of behavior the organization rewards. It's perfectly appropriate in interview situations to ask such questions as "Who succeeds at this company?" "What accomplishments are celebrated here?" or "How do you determine what's a failure?"

What kind of corporate culture best matches your personality? If you haven't thought about this before, now's the time to give it some consideration. Think about the cultures of past organizations you've worked in and review your performance at each one. This can help you predict whether you're headed for a clash at your next job.

If you don't receive an offer, it could be for any of a range of reasons. No one can be a perfect fit for every job, so leave yourself some margin for error. Write to each person you met in the hiring process; express your high regard for them and their organization and your hope that they'll consider you should another opening arise. If you had your heart set on the position, keep your name in front of these folks by corresponding periodically. One way to do this without seeming overly aggressive or pushy is to occasionally pass along an article of interest or a note of congratulation at a promotion or achievement of some milestone.

SECOND INTERVIEWS

The issue of culture fit takes center stage in a second interview. Your background and experience were your ticket to this round; now interviewers will be judging you on the "fit" issues just described, plus how well you might represent the company.

It's tempting to let your guard down in second interviews. Don't. Yes, interviewers must be very interested in you because they asked you back. But they will be listening carefully to everything you say, looking for reasons not to hire you.

To successfully navigate a second interview, think of yourself as already in the position you're seeking. You must exude confidence, so look and play the part. If asked to comment on a particular aspect of the organization, don't be afraid to offer an opinion, if you have one. Hiring managers and peers who are close to an issue are interested in the perspective of outsiders. Moreover, they need to see whether you are an independent thinker and whether you can support an organization's values, goals, and vision. Think through your answer strategically. If you aren't ready for the position and its challenges, it will show.

GROUP INTERVIEWS

If you make the cut, the employer may arrange a group interview to make sure you'll fit in with the rest of the management team. Given their dynamics, these meetings can be difficult, so expect to feel some extra stress. People will be watching to see how you think on your feet. As a daylong meeting with a group proceeds, it's natural to become more relaxed, but you must stay on your toes. You can take comfort in knowing that interviewers understand how tough these meetings can be, and some will be rooting for you to succeed.

In a group dynamic, you'll probably have less time to frame your answers, so be sure to think about the reasons behind the questions and what kind of response is being sought. It's helpful to prepare ahead of time by listing the traits associated with the position you're seeking and rehearsing how you'll demonstrate them in the meeting. Practice in advance with three or four friends or relatives with different personalities. Have them replicate a group-interview situation by asking a series of questions without pausing in between. Seek feedback on what impresses them and why.

You'll want to keep the conversation flowing, so ask timely, relevant questions. One way to ensure smooth transitions is to end your responses to questions by asking interviewers a related question. You also can lower your anxiety and confirm you're on the right track by asking follow-up queries, like "Is this the answer you were seeking?" or "Did I address the issue for you?"

NEGOTIATING YOUR PAY OFFER

Once you've received a job offer, don't think the courtship is over. In her book, *Job Offer! A How-to Negotiation Guide* (JIST Publishing, 2000), author Maryanne L. Wegerbauer convincingly argues that negotiation is an extension of the interview process. Employers are likely to be evaluating your negotiating skills, particularly if you're at the executive level.

Like a couple examining the details of their wedding more seriously than their long-term prospects for a successful marriage, many candidates get caught up in the dynamics of the negotiation process. Rather than seeing it as the foundation for a long-term relationship, it becomes an end in itself.

Start by doing your homework. To get a good idea of what you're worth in the job market, research the going rate for professionals at your level in your field. There's a wealth of information on current compensation on the Internet. Check out the salary data and articles about negotiating available on CareerJournal.com. Two other websites to visit for reliable pay information are www.Salaryexpert.com and www.JobStar.org. Other good resources include professional associations, magazines, business and professional journals, and association websites. Recruiters also can help you learn about current pay trends. Keep in mind that companies may want to maintain internal pay-scale equity, so do your homework on potential employers as well. Compensation practices vary widely.

Once you know what you're worth, listen to the employer's offer. Get it in writing if possible. Don't be the first to mention money. If an interviewer presses you to disclose your salary history or what you hope to make, deflect the question by asking, "What's the salary range for this job?" Another tactic is to cite a respected source. For example: "I'll expect to earn a competitive salary. The American Hospital Association says the average annual salary range for a senior communications manager is between $80,000 and $95,000."

What makes a good negotiator? Preparation and a willingness to understand the other side's needs. Adopting a win–win approach works best. Talking first about the points on which you both can agree will foster a constructive discussion. Stress "we" rather than "I."

Ms. Wegerbauer suggests that you assess the person you'll be negotiating with and adopt an appropriate communication style. While some degree of disagreement is inevitable, you can take steps to lessen conflict. Ms. Wegerbauer recommends using conditional language to soften your message. For example, she says, never react to a proposal with a flat "No." You'll have more success if you, instead, pause to thoughtfully consider what was just said, then respond: "That is not going to work." Then follow up with: "I understand your concerns" or another appropriate phrase. Ms. Wegerbauer suggests using these other helpful transitions:

- "Generally . . ."
- "These are my problems . . ."
- "What if/in lieu of . . ."
- "What is the opportunity for . . . ?"

It's important to bring up any nonnegotiable points early on. Remember, if you don't ask for it, you won't get it. But beware of giving the impression you're impatient or greedy. Be ready to justify that what you're asking for is fair and reasonable.

If you feel you're at a disadvantage because your unemployment has dragged on, a few tactics can help your cause. Silence is a potent one. Former *Wall Street Journal* columnist Hal Lancaster tells a story about a professional who'd been advised not to mention pay issues until the prospective employer made the first move. By not bringing up the issue, the candidate initially was offered $2,000 above what he'd expected. This stunned him into momentary silence. Nature abhors a vacuum. Interpreting the silence as disapproval, the hiring manager heaped another $2,000 onto his offer.

There's more to compensation than just a paycheck, and pay packages for senior executives can be intricate. Stock options and bonuses can play a valuable role in your compensation package. They might include short-term cash incentives and long-term stock-option or stock-grant incentive programs. Performance objectives and vesting schedules vary.

If you'll receive equity, know the size of typical grants for executives in your position and company sector. Many pay surveys provide bonus or total compensation amounts in addition to salary. The size of a grant varies depending on a company's stage and whether it's public. A pre-IPO company is likely to award more options than a large established public company because there's greater risk these incentives may not appreciate in value. Typically, the more critical you are to the company, the more ownership you receive. Since incentive payouts can fluctuate with the economy, look at two or three years' worth of survey data and average the amounts.

Ask about the rules governing the stock-option plan: When can you exercise the options? How soon are they vested? Can you buy and sell them at the same time or do you have to exercise and hold? For how long?

Valuing the stock-option package can be the trickiest part of the negotiating process. Different kinds of options will have different tax implications that can affect their value. You can get help understanding the basics on the Internet at www.mystockoptions.com. But bear in mind that you may need the help of a financial planner, accountant, or lawyer.

Don't focus so much on the number of options you're offered as their value. The most popular method for valuing options is the Black-Scholes method, and there are various calculators available online that can help. One is Robert's Online Option Pricer, created by Dr. Robert Lum and hosted by Intrepid Technology Inc., a Mountain View, California, consulting firm. Its website is: www.intrepid.com/~robertl/option-pricer1.html

When negotiating your deal, consider other items as well. The value of noncash compensation elements, such as benefits and perquisites, can be surprisingly high. Many professional or trade organizations and publications determine the prevalence of benefits and perquisites when conducting annual compensation surveys, so you may be able to learn what other professionals in your field or industry are receiving. The following items can typically be negotiated by executives at the offer stage:

BENEFITS

- Medical, dental, disability, and other insurance plans
- Tuition reimbursement
- Company match of a 401(k) or other retirement plan
- Vacation time

PERQUISITES

- Company car
- Parking
- Country-club membership
- Health-club membership
- PC or laptop computer
- Cell phone
- Home use of company long-distance service
- First-class air tickets
- Spouse travel
- Sports/theatre tickets
- Professional association fees

Additionally, it isn't uncommon for executive candidates to arrange for no- or low-cost loans, such as low-cost mortgages (particularly for relocating candidates) or even low-cost education loans.

If you've been unemployed for any length of time, you're also likely to be interested in such employment terms and conditions as severance and change-in-control provisions. Other job- or income-protection provisions that can be negotiated include an employment contract, outplacement assistance, golden-parachute entitlements, salary-continuation plan, supplemental long-term disability insurance, supplemental retirement plans, and post-retirement consulting.

SHOULD YOU SETTLE FOR LESS?

Many job hunters wonder about this issue. Those who have been unemployed for long periods often are very willing to accept a lower-level job or reduced pay just to get a paycheck again. To them, their choice seems like a win-win for the employer. What manager wouldn't want to hire an experienced person who's willing to work at something he or she has probably done at earlier stages of their career? The answer is, ironically, very few. There are several reasons.

First, bosses are concerned that as soon as the job market improves, executives and professionals who accepted lesser jobs will leave for better offers. Although candidates are loath to admit this to a prospective employer, some privately confess they'd change jobs quickly if something better came along. With a mortgage and other bills to pay, the new hire who wouldn't skip out for a better-paying, more challenging position is either very loyal or has other income. "Gun-shy" put it well:

I was out of work for almost a year before I finally landed something, albeit at a 35 percent pay cut and in an area in which I'm not particularly interested. As luck would have it, after being at the job for three days, I now have two other strong job possibilities that may force me to consider leaving after only a week or so. This is a great problem to have after thinking for a while that my career was finished, but it is still stressful.

Employers also prefer not to hire overqualified workers because they fear these employees will get bored doing something that's beneath their skill level. This isn't necessarily true; some executives and professionals want to take a step back, whether to gain more balance in their lives, to ease their work pressure, or for other reasons.

Prospective employers think that one will accept the job and keep looking for a better one. I have advised all that I don't plan to do that. I am very fortunate that my husband has two incomes and I was able to take early retirement from my prior employer. But I am never sure if prospective employers believe me. I have reached a point in life where I don't want the stress and aggravation that I have had in the past, so I am willing to take less money. —VB

Employers fear, too, that overqualified employees may not work well with younger people in positions above them; may be too aggressive about getting ahead; won't be as interested in contributing as a younger person being promoted into the role; will be a drain on company benefits; and so on.

Ted Martin, president and CEO of recruiter Martin Partners in Chicago, says candidates who are willing to work for less present a paradigm dilemma for employers, because often such job hunters can do the jobs well but don't like them, so they may act in ways that bring about a dismissal. He warns such candidates: "You're saying, 'Put me in a rut—I'll love it.'"

EXAMINE YOUR MOTIVES FOR ACCEPTING LESS

So, why *would* you want to be paid less and work at something you've done already? Have you lost confidence in your ability to land work at your most recent level because of a long bout of unemployment? Do you think no one wants you? Does this seem like the easiest way out of a bad situation? Look at your reasons and decide if you are casting around for a solution to end your job hunt. Next, realize that you may have become depressed or discouraged and may need to seek help to restore your confidence. Remember, there is no easy way out of a job transition.

Your job target should be at the right level for your experience and abilities—"your age and stage," as one career counselor calls it. Make sure your résumé is targeted to this level and that you are aiming for such opportunities. If you find that larger companies aren't interested, look for openings at smaller concerns that may need someone seasoned; someone with the wisdom that comes only from experience.

Examine your attitude: make sure that you're positive and upbeat with networking contacts and employers. Dwell on what you can offer, not on your misgivings. Stay abreast of technology and look at how you can use it when discussing potential alliances. By the same token, be sure your wardrobe and appearance don't seem old-fashioned. If you aren't already working out, start doing so, to optimize your health and your appearance of vigor and vitality; employers will be more confident that you're up to the challenge of a high-level role.

PLAYING THE LOW-PAY CARD SUCCESSFULLY

Perhaps, however, you sincerely want to scale back, or you are consciously seeking a lower-paying job as a tactic to help you get hired faster. Some job hunters, such as Julius A., view this approach as an effective interim step to get them to the next level. He wrote:

The real trick to getting a new job is . . . be willing to work for less through the tough times. This sounds trite, but since I lowered my yearly salary requirements, I have started to get real interviews and people highly interested in fighting for me. The positions involve basic work—back to my roots as a controller in some cases—but if they want you and you like them, it gets you through. I did this many years ago when I went from $100,000 to $65,000 for one year and wound up at $120,000 a year later when things got better. So do not give up hope, and do not think you can't work for less.

Here are a few strategies that can help you to overcome employers' misconceptions and convince them to hire you for a lower-level role:

- Be the solution. Point out what you can do to help an employer solve a problem. Perhaps you are sufficiently experienced to do two jobs at a company; if so, point this out during interviews.
- Say you'll take the job at a lower salary but want to prove your worth and be considered for more responsibility. In this case, ask for most of your pay in the form of performance incentives in return for actual revenue contributions you know you can make (be sure to get such an agreement in writing).
- Sign a contract saying that you will stay for a certain period or repay your salary.
- Have a convincing reason for wanting to work at this level. Perhaps you are returning to the job market after an absence and need to lower your initial expectations because of the gap on your résumé.
- Offer to do the job as a contractor, working fewer hours than the employer originally envisioned.

Remember, the best job isn't always the one that pays the most. Consider the job content and your career prospects. Will you have enough autonomy, authority, and scope to accomplish your objectives? Do you subscribe to the firm's values and operating style? Do you respect its leaders? And will the job move you along to the next level? Consider the career opportunity, position, company and industry, your lifestyle, and intangible issues, such as your potential coworkers, company culture, and their values and ethics. Also take into account your future earnings potential, current or future equity potential, deferred compensation, benefits, and relocation package.

STARTING A NEW JOB ON A GOOD FOOTING

Ideally, before you accept an offer you'll have done a lot of what lawyers call "due diligence"—thorough research into the company's current situation and recent past. In addition to getting all the facts and figures, get to know as many people as you can, as well as you can. Meet them outside of the office environment; play golf or have dinner with them.

Once you've accepted an offer, it's a good idea to create a training program for your first months on the job. It should be a detailed document, in writing, with a schedule. Spend time getting to know different aspects of the job. For example, a CEO might spend a week at a plant and another at a sales conference to learn in depth about the organization's strengths and weaknesses. The most successful professionals have a deep understanding of the business they're in and get to know the employees and, especially, the customers.

• • •

No matter how much you may want to, don't oversell yourself to hiring managers in the interviewing process. There should be as low a level of expectation as possible when you first start a job. You'll feel less pressure, and you'll look better once you exceed expectations. If you're not the right person for the job, you and your supervisors will know soon enough.

LATE-NIGHT REFLECTIONS ON MY UNEMPLOYMENT

- Looking Back from a Distance

- Lessons Learned

- An Opportunity for Transformation

- What I Wish I Had Known Before the Pink Slip

- Networking Is Always Necessary

- Sharing What You've Learned

December 4

If you'd asked me eight long months ago where I'd end up after my job
search, I wouldn't have predicted this outcome. I'm now the chief information officer and associate to the chief operating officer of a $100 million non-
profit human-services organization with 3,000 employees in more than 150
programs in 9 states. From health care to performing arts to small-business
incubation, the depth and breadth of its programming are impressive.

It's been two months since I began my new job and, having gained some distance, I've been reflecting on my experience. Looking back at my job search,
I see two processes. There's a superficial, mechanical one; that's the external search—the research, résumés, phone calls, recruiters, and interviews.
There's also a deeper, spiritual process; that's the real search—the process
of self-discovery, transformation, and reinvention.

At the risk of losing the more jaded readers, I want to tell those of you who
are unemployed that you have a remarkable opportunity to transform your-
selves. My own transformation required that I circle the globe of self-
identity, only to return to a spot not far from where I'd started. I wrote off
the entire nonprofit sector and ultimately returned to it. In the process I
was transformed, because I'd learned that I actually could do what I wanted
to do and, better still, I'd found a place to do it. The answer I was looking
for appeared in quiet and calm. There was no panic or doubt in the process.

I'm sure people are transformed in different ways. While I was unemployed, I
spent time searching for meaning: What am I supposed to be doing? Where
is my place in the world? What is my responsibility to others? Should I really
listen to a recruiter? The struggle helped me to re-examine my beliefs about
the world and myself.

I'd sought psychic sustenance from unemployed comrades. I now miss the
sense of belonging that I felt while I was struggling. While misery may love
company, so does hope. I had the pleasure of seeing some of my fellow job
seekers at their very best—when they were most human, humble, coura-
geous, and kind. I felt a bond with even those people I never met—those who
posted messages on various bulletin boards or simply existed for me as
ideas. We were bound together as partners in a most difficult adventure.

THE PHOENIX EFFECT

During my experience, my employed friends drifted to the back of my consciousness. Nothing personal—they were part of "them." Employed acquaintances and strangers were even more abstract to me; they were simply targets of my sales calls or, worse, vaguely alien—mere shadows.

But now I am employed again. Transformed. Reinvented. The change should be striking. Life is less dramatic now, and that's perhaps what's most dramatic. I now am too busy to ponder symbolism and meaning, but I have the luxury of wondering when I'll find the time to buy shoes, get an oil change, or exercise. With my family's and my own basic needs met, I must remain vigilant. I must defend against being reduced—by the tyrannies of stability and routine—to a bag of minor aches, pains, and complaints.

Now that I'm employed again, my fellow employed people are in sharp focus. Since I feel lucky to have a job, and especially one I love, I'm amazed to rediscover how many people are either indifferent about their jobs or actually dislike them. They've allowed themselves to be reduced to bags of minor aches, pains, and complaints.

Employed or not, life is hard. But we have a chance to see it differently.

GOING FORWARD

Regarding the mechanics of the job search, my take-away is that you can never let a potential employer smell your desperation; it's completely off-putting. I knew this when I was an actor but somehow I'd forgotten it. The key to getting parts was to not want them. I'd walk into an audition praying that I wouldn't get the job, and I would get it. A simpler, less twisted version of this maxim: be comfortable with where you are and who you are, and people will be drawn to you.

There are also a couple of things I wish I'd known before I was laid off. First, networking isn't vulgar. I never really understood that before. I'm now committed to the careful feeding and watering of my network. I'll try to stay connected during good times and support those who are going through hard times so that I'll have more folks to lean on (and feel better about doing so) when I hit another rough patch.

The second major lesson I must partially credit to author Tom Peters, who acquainted me with the concept in one of his books. Only after I was unemployed did it strike me as a meaningful strategy. It's this: Going forward, I'll critically view each work activity and project I engage in to determine how I can maximize value for my employer and myself, and how I can grow from the experience. If it isn't worth doing, I'll find a way to get it done quickly or not do it at all. In this way, I'll build a solid record of accomplishments and when I need to redo my résumé again, not have to wonder quite as much about how I spent my time.

Thanks and good luck to you all. I think about you often.

LOOKING BACK FROM A DISTANCE

While CareerJournal.com often publishes articles by job seekers, it's rare that we publish a story before the writer finds a job. Tim's series was different—a work in progress, let's say—and while his account was suspenseful, it also filled a need in the job-hunting community. Before we knew it, other job seekers were chronicling their searches on our discussion board. Several found work almost simultaneously with Tim, and some have continued to write in to the site months after the series ended.

A community developed. Readers wanted to participate in a dialogue with each other via our website. So much shame is attached to being unemployed; they wanted to feel they weren't the only ones who were having difficulty finding work. We received comments on the "Tim Johnston Discussion" from candidates young and old, entry-level to executive, inside and outside the United States. As Erik wrote in:

There are thousands of people experiencing the same ups and downs of what it takes to find a job in today's marketplace. Psychologically, knowing I'm far from alone provides a boost as I sit at home listening to the phone not ringing and watching my email inbox in futility as I wait for some correspondence from a "Sir or Madam."

More than a few career counselors, recruiters, and employers offered advice—and sometimes, tough love. Criticism was welcome; some readers even blasted away at Tim, which he didn't seem to mind:

Tim's latest article about job-hunting online is totally useless. A lengthy dissertation about what doesn't work should clearly—to be of any use to job-seekers—clearly (I know I repeat myself—guess why?) point in the right direction when it comes to advice on "how to do things right, the first time." This is clearly not the case in this article. —inc sense

Such comments would provoke a dialogue in their own right. But most inspiring was the free-flowing and generous support our participants gave each other. When someone reported that they'd achieved a milestone—an interview, offer, or meeting with a helpful networking contact—the others applauded. If someone discussed a disappointment, the others empathized. No one was jealous or resentful of another's success. Clearly, among the lessons learned from the series was the fact that job seekers need to connect with each other on a meaningful level, either in cyberspace or at support-group meetings. Spouses and well-meaning friends aren't enough. The search process can be so dispiriting that only by supporting and praising each other can job seekers maintain the confidence so necessary for eventual success.

LESSONS LEARNED

That said, let's examine what Tim—and by extension, we—learned during the months of job searching.

- **First, Job Hunting Isn't Designed to Humiliate Us Personally:** Those of us who take rejection well don't suffer as much as those who believe that it's personal—"I could tell the interviewer rejected me because he didn't like me." Job hunters are playing the odds. Everyone's number comes up differently, but you have to keep buying the lottery tickets—finding opportunities, going on interviews—to stay in the game. As Uptown123 (who, incidentally, also found a new job during this period) wrote after he landed his position:

Let me hammer home the point that there is absolutely nothing wrong with any of us. Like other people have said, I also was asking myself if I would ever work again. In reality, a gut part of me knew that was a rhetorical question, and it really is. The economy just has its resources allocated all wrong, and it will right itself. It must. The problem simply doesn't lie with us or our abilities.

- **You Need to Create Your Own Luck:** Nothing in a job hunt happens purely by accident. Perhaps it seems that way: you run into a school chum you haven't seen in years who happens to work in the industry you're targeting; you visit a website on a whim and see a posting that's ideal for you; you send a letter to an employer on the spur of the moment and get a request to come interview the next week. Even Tim's letter in response to his future employer's posting seemed somewhat whimsical.

But everyone who reports such a happenstance must be prepared and open to the opportunity to take advantage of it. Remember, the formula for job-search success (and many other types of success, too) is: luck + preparation = opportunity. Tim was prepared, so he recognized immediately that the opening he read about was something he wanted. Stay open to all opportunities: to talk with people you don't know; to make a chance encounter meaningful; to be inquisitive, even if there seems to be no immediate payback.

AN OPPORTUNITY FOR TRANSFORMATION

From these lessons, we can see that clearly, in the long run, your attitude about who you are and your future is more important than the nuts and bolts of job hunting. Everyone can learn to write a good résumé and cover letter and find the right websites to visit. But it's when you are mentally ready and stimulated by the job-search challenge, that the rest falls into place.

Perhaps this mental turnaround is what many newly employed people mean when they say they were transformed by their experience. They changed. In the end, they knew how to apply serendipity in their lives. They knew what they wanted and what ultimately was most meaningful to them. They used this knowledge to find something better to do professionally. They had gone through one of the hardest experiences of their lives and come out on the other side stronger and more resourceful. Change is painful, and, cliché or not, the greatest gains come through the greatest pain.

Many job seekers start the search process as victims. Their layoffs were unfair; their bosses were cowards; the world owes them. They end it as victors, in charge of their lives and their futures. One can say that a job transition is about control—learning that the only person in charge of your life is you. Although Tim doesn't come out and say it directly, you can spot this transformation in his writing. No one really wants to be dependent on a boss or an employer for a paycheck. We all feel better knowing that if our companies are acquired and our positions are eliminated, we have the ability to take care of ourselves. If we've done this once, we know we can do it again.

WHAT I WISH I'D KNOWN BEFORE THE PINK SLIP

What will you learn from your job loss and subsequent period of unemployment? The following, we hope:

- **Change Is the Only Constant You Can Count On in Business:** If you haven't adopted this mindset by now, you probably won't be very valuable (or remain long) at your next employer. Look for ways to adapt to constant change in the work world. What you do today likely isn't what you did yesterday, nor what you'll do tomorrow. New jobs are being created constantly; keep evolving to fit them.

- **Bitterness and Resentment Will Keep You on the Sidelines:** A positive, flexible attitude is essential. Employers can spot negativity like the plague.

- **Outside Factors Reign:** You will remain at your next job only as long as economic conditions and supply and demand cooperate. If your skills aren't needed, it's adios. Look for developing areas and help your employer capitalize on them. Keep doing this and you'll keep creating work for yourself.

- **Think of Yourself as a Company of One:** Tim vowed to look at his work activities with a critical eye, focusing primarily on those that would get him to the next step. If you owned a company, would you spend your time on non-revenue-generating work or on getting your product into the hands of customers and bringing in revenues?

  Tim says this advice came courtesy of management guru Tom Peters, who champions the Me, Inc. career-management philosophy. CareerJournal.com once asked Mr. Peters for his single best piece of career advice. His response: "Assume that the dreaded post-reengineering pink slip landed on your desk at 5 P.M. today, and then take a cold, cruel future employer's look at the state of your résumé now."

He goes so far as to recommend that anyone currently employed should take tomorrow off to rewrite their resumes, then ask a headhunter or career counselor to review it. If it doesn't light that person's candle, take a look at what you're working on and say, "How can I change this project so that it's worth bragging about tomorrow?" In short, you're only as good as your portfolio of projects.

NETWORKING IS ALWAYS NECESSARY

In hindsight, and not surprisingly, Tim says his most valuable lesson is that networking isn't vulgar. Some folks do regard it as a dirty word, and when done badly, it is. Contacts shouldn't feel as though they're on the end of a sales transaction, or that they're being used, unappreciated, or badgered. Networking requires treating them with the utmost respect, never overstepping boundaries, and keeping the stakes low. Don't abuse your network, or you may risk losing it.

Referrals are the lifeblood of networking, and your "referrer" has gone out on a limb for you. When you call the person you were referred to, be up front about why you're calling. Such individuals should never feel duped or somehow pressured into helping you because of your mutual friend's OK. Also, networking isn't another word for gabbing; if you're seeking assistance, listen to what contacts say, then thank them appropriately—and take their advice.

Most important, don't let dust collect on your Rolodex. We should all be committed, like Tim, to the "careful feeding and watering" of our network. Calling someone out of the blue is more difficult than if you've made periodic contact over the months. As one discussion-board participant told the group: "Don't wait until you're unemployed to start networking."

The writer was a former aerospace industry vice president in the San Francisco Bay Area who'd once taken nine months to land a new job. He learned how to network at Forty Plus, a national job-search organization with local chapters. His story offers much helpful advice about readiness and job hunting and reiterates the importance of staying connected:

I planned for my next job search the day I started my new job. In my previous position, I concentrated more on the internal elements of the business. This limited my external contacts. After I lost my job, my network was limited. My job-search plan was not only to land a new job but also to ensure that the position included the ability to expand my network as part of performing the job's responsibilities.

I accepted a position as the general manager of a small company. My responsibilities included managing the internal operations and also business development. This provided me with the opportunity not only to build the reputation of the company but also to showcase my abilities outside of the company. I took an active role in establishing the company's vendor and subcontractor base and worked with the customers. Eventually, although my division was performing well, the parent company failed, resulting in its closure and leaving me to conduct another job search. This time it was much easier. I had established a solid reputation outside the company, which provided several consulting opportunities and eventually my current position. Networking is the key, but family and friends aren't going to help you land that next job. The network of suppliers, subcontractors, customers, and competitors will. —Al H.

Don't burn bridges with former colleagues at your past employer; you never know when you might need them. Find out what they're doing now. More than anyone else, these people know your value and may be willing to recommend you in their new companies. Contacts from a past professional life also can serve as personal benchmarks. By speaking with them, you can see how much you've changed and that your transition was more helpful than you realized.

Networking with recruiters will likely be easier once you're reemployed. Now you're a more valuable commodity to them. Update the ones you contacted during your transition on where you "landed." Call or send notes to those specializing in your field, function, or local area and offer to assist them in future searches. If a recruiter contacts you about a new position, always return the call, even if you're not interested in a move. Listen to the description of the opportunity; volunteer possible candidates, if you know of any. Now's the time to build good relationships with headhunters.

SHARING WHAT YOU'VE LEARNED

Are you so grateful and relieved to be employed that you'd like to give back some of what you've received from others? Perhaps your transformation has changed you in deeper ways; you now believe, for instance, that meaning in life comes more from helping others for no personal gain than from how many hours you put in at the office.

Start by writing to everyone who helped with your search process. Thank them for their assistance, tell them where you're working, and offer to help if they ever need it. If it seems appropriate, say a few words about how the experience has altered your life and thinking.

Get in touch with local job-search support groups and ask how you might volunteer. Perhaps you can arrange for an evening speaker, mentor members of the group, be a substitute chairperson, or simply participate during meeting discussions. Some former job hunters have been so moved by their own difficulties and eventual rebound that they have stayed involved with such groups for decades. Others have changed careers so they work with job seekers. After retiring or taking severance packages from former employers, they have gone to work at the outplacement firms that helped them to pick up the pieces after a layoff.

Try to remain true to your vow to continue networking. It's remarkable how many candidates forget the importance of staying connected; after their next layoff, they kick themselves for neglecting their contacts. Of course, it goes without saying that one of the best ways to give back is to help job hunters who receive your name from referrals. Don't ever be too busy to network with a candidate.

Tim continues to stay in touch with the discussion group, occasionally offering his two cents. His stories, which remain on CareerJournal.com, keep showing others that there's a light at the end of the tunnel.

• • •

No doubt you've gained new knowledge about yourself and the process of reemployment. While your volunteer activities with other job seekers may not have Tim's breadth, just being available to one person can be a gift.

CAREER RESOURCES

BOOKS

Beyond Juggling: Rebalancing Your Busy Life by Kurt Sandholtz (Berrett Koehler Publishers Inc., 2002)

The New Perfect Résumé by Tom Jackson (Doubleday Main Street Books, 2003)

What Color Is Your Parachute? by Richard N. Bolles (Ten Speed Press, 2003) (visit the companion website, www.jobhuntersbible.com)

Guide to Internet Job Searching, 2002–2003, by Margaret Riley Dikel, Frances E. Roehm, and the Public Library Association (VGM Career Books, 2002)

The Overnight Job Change Strategy by Don Asher (Ten Speed Press, 1993)

The Brand You 50: Fifty Ways to Transform Yourself from an "Employee" into a Brand That Shouts Distinction, Commitment, and Passion! by Tom Peters (Knopf, 2000)

I Don't Know What I Want, but I Know It's Not This: A Step-by-Step Guide to Finding Gratifying Work by Julie Jansen (Penguin Books, 2003)

Fearless Interviewing by Marky Stein (Writers Club Press, 2001)

Job Offer! A How-to Negotiation Guide by Maryanne L. Wegerbauer (JIST Publishing, 2000)

WEBSITES

GENERAL

CareerJournal.com	www.careerjournal.com
JobHuntersBible.com	www.jobhuntersbible.com
The Riley Guide	www.rileyguide.com

COMPANY RESEARCH

U.S. Securities and Exchange Commission's Electronic Data Gathering, Analysis, and Retrieval system (EDGAR)	www.sec.gov/edgar.shtml
Hoover's, Inc.	www.hoovers.com
Thomas Register	www.thomasregister.com
Forbes	www.forbes.com

NETWORKING

Yahoo! Inc.'s PeopleSearch	http://people.yahoo.com
Addresses.com	www.addresses.com
CareerJournal.com's Calendar of Career Events	www.careerjournal.com/calendar/index.html

ONLINE NETWORKING

Vault	www.vault.com
Lycos Communities	http://clubs.lycos.com/live/Directory/welcome.asp
MSN Groups	http://groups.msn.com
America Online (for AOL members only)	www.aol.com

EXECUTIVE RECRUITERS

Kennedy Information Inc.	www.kennedyinfo.com

JOB FAIRS

JobEXPO.com
(American Job Fairs, Inc.)

www.americanjobfairs.com

Career Fairs Global Inc. (CFG)

www.cfg-inc.com

HRLive

www.hrlive.com

Jobhunt.org

www.job-hunt.org/fairs.shtml

CAREER ADVISERS AND COACHES

Association of Career
Professionals International

www.acpinternational.org

International Coach Federation

www.coachfederation.org

The National Board for
Certified Counselors

www.nbcc.org

NONPROFIT JOBS

Opportunity Knocks

www.opportunitynocs.org

Idealist

www.idealist.org

Nonprofit Career Network

www.nonprofitcareer.com

The Chronicle of Philanthropy

www.philanthropy.com

The Chronicle of
Higher Education

www.chronicle.com

VOLUNTEER OPPORTUNITIES

VolunteerMatch

www.volunteermatch.org

VolunteerAmerica

www.volunteeramerica.net

NONPROFIT NEWS, INFORMATION, AND AFFILIATES

Nonprofit Tech	www.nonprofit-tech.org
Internet Nonprofit Center	www.nonprofits.org
The NonProfit Times	www.nptimes.com
The Nonprofit Genie	www.genie.org
GuideStar	www.guidestar.org
Leader to Leader Institute (formerly The Drucker Foundation)	www.pfdf.org
The Foundation Center	www.fdncenter.org
The Roberts Enterprise Development Fund	www.redf.org
Alliance for Nonprofit Management	www.allianceonline.org
Nonprofit Notes	www.inom.org/npnotes.htm

INDEX

Email address book, keeping your, 14
Emotional reactions to job loss
    children's, 131
    first reactions, 2, 6, 7
    how to handle, 111-12, 114, 124, 132
    spouses' and partners', 120–21, 123–24
    stages, 124
Empathy with job loser, 125
Employees
    "fit" with employers, 21, 140, 161–62
    overqualified, 167–68
Employers. See also Hiring managers
    blaming for career dissatisfaction, 150
    cold calls to prospective, 3
    considering needs of, 28
    criticizing, 15
    employee "fit" with, 21, 140, 161–62
    imagining being, and hiring yourself, 45
    obtaining support from previous, 9, 11
    phone calls to prospective, 48
    reluctance to hire overqualified
        employees, 167–70
Employment ads. See Job ads
Enthusiasm for job searching, 138, 155
ExecuNet, 101
Experience. See Job experience

F

Failure to find a job
    coping with, 106, 108–9, 111
    determining reasons for, 112–13
Family members. See also Children; Parents;
        Spouses and partners
    obtaining contacts from, 4–5
    responding to hurtful comments by,
        109–10, 133
    seeing, during unemployment, 118
    sharing job loss news with, 69
    support from, after job loss, 2–3
    ways they can help, 133
Fax machines for job searching, 12
Fearfulness during job search, 122
    avoiding, 126
    of children, 131
    money worries, 126–27
Federal government jobs, 143
Feedback from interviewers, 80
Feelings. See Emotional reactions to job loss;

or names of specific emotions
Finances. See Personal finances
Finding a job. See Job search
Firing. See Job loss
Forbes.com, 61
Forty Plus, 101
Franklin, Benjamin, 161
Friends, 14, 69
    calling when depressed, 110
    finding supportive, 131–32
    while employed vs. unemployed, 173
Functional résumés, 43–44
    when to use, 27

G

Gatekeepers, bypassing, 48
Generalists, 20
Goals. See also Career goals
    differences between spouses over, 129–30
    need to focus on, 112
    at networking meetings, 15
    non-job-search, 115
    steps in achieving, 113
Good fortune during job search, 118, 176
Government jobs, 143
Grieving a lost job, 6
    stages, 124
Group events, networking at, 101–2
Group interviews, 80, 163–64
Guide to Internet Job Searching, 2002–2003
    (Dikel and Roehm), 26
Gut instinct, 33

H

Headhunters. See Recruiters
Health insurance, 12, 30, 71
Help, 113. See also Advice; Career counseling
        services
    counseling, 111–12
    from friends, 131–32
    from your children, 131
Helping others, 179–80
Helpless feelings of spouses and partners,
        127–30
"Hidden job market," 103
Hiring managers. See also Employers

decision-making about taking, 160–61
taking first one, 73
Job requirements in ads, 155
Jobs
best, 170
how to get lower-paying, 169–70
how to start new, 170
ideal, 162
knowing if they are right, 160–61
negotiable terms and conditions of, 167
Job satisfaction, 139, 140
Job search. *See also* Career management;
Failure to find a job; Interviewing;
Older job seekers; Résumés
attitude transformation during, 176–77
changing direction midstream, 148–50,
153–54
creating structure for, 113, 114
duration to expect, 13
effectiveness of job fairs in, 97–98
equation for success, 92
events to attend, 100
goal changing during, 136–38
hitting the wall during, 105–18
lessons learned by Tim Johnston, 175–76
link between passion and success, 138–39
making your own luck during, 118
numbers game, 81, 95
online, 51-64
positive affirmations, 111
questions to consider, 141
during a recession, 4
spouses' and partners' role during, 119–34
strategy, 13–14, 106
targeted, 48–49
techniques, 5
two processes in, 172
using search engines, 60–61, 62
when to begin, 9
winding up, 157–70
Job-search-assistance programs, 12
Job-search groups, 110, 114, 174–75
staying connected with, after
reemployment, 180
in your local area, 59
Job-search networks, 101
Job-search scams, 103–4
Job security, loss of belief in, 122
Job sharing, 31

Job skills. *See* Skills
Job switching, 148–50
prior to career switching, 151–52
within same field or industry, 151
Johnston, Tim, 2. *See also* Rosenson, Claire
Judgmental questions, responses to, 109–10,
111, 133

K

Keywords
cover letters, 47
résumé, 10, 37–38, 47, 62
Kübler-Ross, Elisabeth, 124

L

Lawyers, consulting about severance pay
packages, 11
Layoff. *See* Job loss
Learning experiences, preparing stories
about, 88
Leverage. *See* Bargaining power
Loans, negotiating with employers for, 167
Loneliness during job search, 132, 174
Luck during job search, 118, 176
Lying to get a job, 162

M

Marketing yourself, 112
thinking of yourself as a business, 29,
170, 177
using résumés, 45
Marriages. *See* Spouses and partners
Maslow, Abraham, 139
MBAjobs.net, 52
Mergers, 7, 8
Mindset
improving your, 111, 114–16
transformation during job searching,
176–77
while interviewing, 81
Misrepresenting yourself to get a job, 162
Mission, finding your, 142
Money. *See also* Personal finances